Tantric Sex

Start Unleashing Your Sexual Potential and Build a True Connection with Your Partner Through Proven Techniques and Meditations to Reach Ultimate Pleasure

Jenny Love

© Copyright 2020 - All rights reserved.

This document is geared towards providing exact and reliable information in regard to the topic and issue covered.

- From a Declaration of Principles which was accepted and approved equally by a Committee of the American Bar Association and a Committee of Publishers and Associations.

In no way is it legal to reproduce, duplicate, or transmit any part of this document in either electronic means or in printed format. All rights reserved.

The information provided herein is stated to be truthful and consistent, in that any liability, in terms of inattention or otherwise, by any usage or abuse of any policies, processes, or directions contained within is the solitary and utter responsibility of the recipient reader. Under no circumstances will any legal responsibility or blame be held against the publisher for any reparation, damages, or monetary loss due to the information herein, either directly or indirectly.

Respective authors own all copyrights not held by the publisher.

The information herein is offered for informational purposes solely and is universal as so. The presentation of the information is without contract or any type of guarantee assurance.

The trademarks that are used are without any consent, and the publication of the trademark is without permission or backing by the trademark owner. All trademarks and brands within this book are for clarifying purposes only and are owned by the owners themselves, not affiliated with this document.

Table of Contents

Introduction 1

Tantra, Getting Started 5

Discover The Chakras (All 7 Chakra) 13

History Of Tantra 19

Tantric Sex Basics 27

Tantric Meditation 31

Benefits of Tantric Sex 39

Tantric Sex in the Relationship and General Tips 47

Tantric Massage 53

Tantric Yoga 61

Tantric Sex And Tantric Sex Positions 67

Feminine Orgasms And Tantra 73

How To Control Ejaculation And Last Longer 81

What Is An Intimate Pussy Massage? 85

Discover Your Own Body And That Of Your Partner 93

Preparing for Tantric Sex – What You Need to do 97

Tricks and Tips 105

Conclusion 109

Introduction

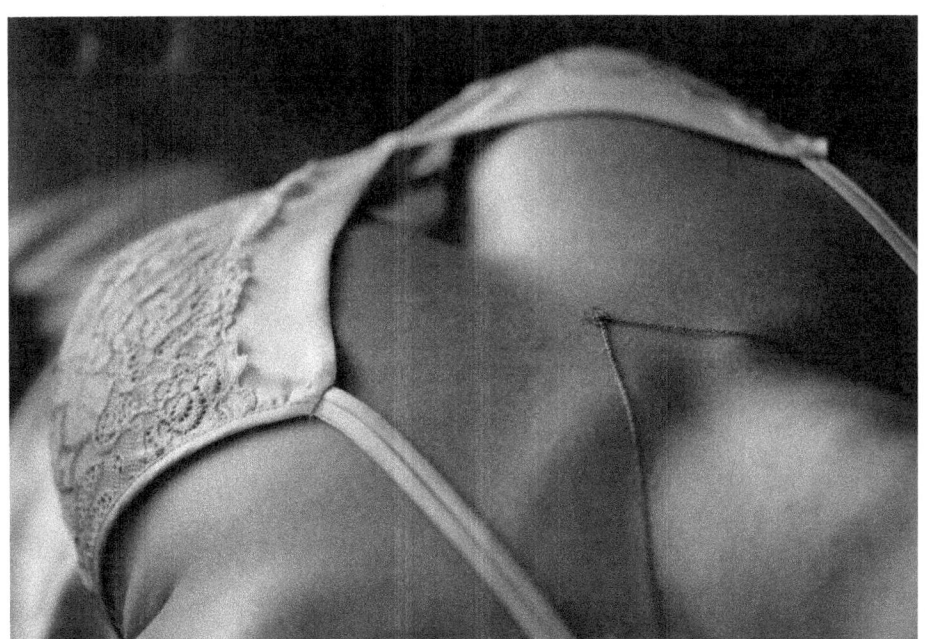

Tantra is a very ancient religious practice originating in India and was formalized in the 11th century. tantric sex is the process of expanding orgasmic feelings by meditating on certain images, breathing deep and hard to control 'tension' in certain places of the body, and focusing on sex to reach higher spiritual experiences.

Tantric sex is not about overtaking the other person. tantric sex is very much about love, mutual expansion, and the journey to becoming one. It is all about energy, intimacy, and beauty.

The desire to begin in a healthy way tantric sex is faith-based. any healthy human being would want to create an atmosphere that can stimulate them sexually, innocently, and calmly.

To begin tantric sex, take a bath before or after making love. The warmth of the water prompts relaxation and sensuality which is a major step on a joyful path then, take some time to breathe slowly and deeply. When your imagination is soothed, you will find it easier to forget and appreciate the surroundings. When you feel relaxed, you are ready for tantric sex, then take your lover with your eyes, hold each other in a loving embrace, the beginning of tantric sex can define the end of first time sex. The inner journey to push your limits is very important, it can mark the beginning of a new type of sensual experience leading you both to a new phase of tantric sex encounter.

Tantra is the Indian word for art, there is a lot to learn about sex in tantric sex and a lot to explore. Sex in tantric sex is not a mundane act, it should be a means to an end, it should be a whole new ritual and journey which can be enjoyed and appreciated with great pleasure.

In tantric sex, remember to relax every muscle in your body, drop your eyelids and listen to the sounds that come out of your body, it is best to use lubricant and to use the pillow when giving head, keep the activities slow, and keep your sexual organ and private parts clean.

Falling in love with tantric sex is not the end of the journey. After you become aroused and stimulated with tantric sex, you must continue your love by focusing on love in all that you do strengthen the bond between yourselves through sensual postures and sex. Reach for each other's hearts and minds with awe-inspiring thoughts, let your hearts be punctured with little bits of love. let your mindfulness grow and expand as if it could never go further anywhere else.

Tantric sex requires presence. Presence is a vital factor in the journey to becoming one with your sexual partner. When you are present, you feel that you are no longer alone and share the moment with your lover. Tantric sex will make you understand that a person's true sexual nature comes out of rejection.

Rejection is the building of your sexual identity, rejection is the explanation for the explosion of sensual fluidity and desire, rejection makes your sexual organs and organs rise with the greatest form of sexual energy. Be rejected and give up everything that you think may kill your sexual experience.

Tantric sex is also a way to give someone the greatest pleasure. Sex in tantric sex is not just about physical pleasure.

Tantra, Getting Started

Tantra is not a religion, albeit Tantric symbology and practices have risen from the beginning of time in all religions and societies. Portrayals of the holy association of the manly and female standards and the non-duality of this "holy internal marriage" can be found as far back as 2000 BC in the Indus Valley development and the old Egyptian kingdom. Tantric standards are innate in otherworldly Judaism (Kabbalah), Christianity, and Sufism. Chinese Taoism is another strand of Tantra.

Tantra most clearly developed in India, somewhere in the range of 300 and 400 CE, when the main Hindu and Buddhist Tantric writings were recorded as graceful illustrations indicating unity and Divine love. These first works were intentionally dark with the goal that no one but starts could get them. Before that time, Tantric lessons were firmly watched and transmitted orally from ace to teach simply after extensive stretches of planning and purification.

Tantra arrived at its peak in the eleventh and twelfth centuries, when it was generally and transparently rehearsed in India. Tantra invalidated the predominant idea that freedom could be achieved uniquely through thorough austerity and by renouncing the world. Tantrikas (tantric yogis) accepted that human experience emerges from the mixed up thought of partition. It pushed festivity of the exotic and, through so doing greatness of the physical.

Tantra has been and still is polished in three principal shapes: the religious convention, the householder custom, and meandering yogis. Though Hinduism had numerous guidelines and laws, including severe divisions of the station, Tantra was non-denominational and could be polished by anybody, even inside everyday life.

In this manner, reflections on weaving, for instance, could be drilled by weavers, as they thought about the interlaced and undifferentiated nature of presence. Simultaneously, interventions on eating, drinking, and lovemaking could be rehearsed by lords and rulers.

With India's intrusion in the thirteenth century came across the board butcher of Tantrics and destruction of their original copies. Tantra went underground, where it has transcendently stayed since. Tantric Buddhism was strikingly safeguarded in the religious communities of Tibet. After the Chinese attack of Tibet, when priests and nuns were killed and original copies wrecked, the individuals who got away have discovered approaches to disperse this learning all the more broadly delicately.

It is standard to separate Tantric ways into two segments. Those where the individual professional works with his/her sexual vitality, for the most part inside, are classified "right-gave" ways or "white Tantra." At that point, there are Tantric methodologies that do include direct sexual contact between affection accomplices, and these are designated "left-gave" Tantra or "red Tantra." As it may, these terms are themselves part of a progressively present-day arrangement of classification.

In the west, today, conventional Tantric practices can be found inside the Tibetan Buddhist custom and using the Kundalini and Kriya yoga schools, which are all right-gave ways. There is additionally the Taoist custom, which has just somewhat been modified, and this is a left-gave way. Daniel Odier was started by Lalita Devi in the Himalayas, in the genealogy of Kasmimir Shaivism.

He instructs the primary practices are sitting contemplation, the "tandava," a type of extremely unpretentious free development. Experts contact an ever-increasing number of refined conditions of the "divine tremoring" a reverberation with the pith of life. Kashmiri vitality knead.

Generally, Tantric experts did not promote themselves, and this is, for the most part, still obvious today. Many exist, especially in India, in the West. However, you will not discover such a large number of Tantric bosses using the web.

The birthplace of the tantric customs is a puzzler, to a great extent because of the scarcity of recorded proof in India from the period when it appears that they originally developed during the Gupta line (320–550 C.E.). This scarcity of proof has prompted a lot of rampant theories concerning the birthplace of these customs. There is no hard proof for the presence of tantric conventions before the mid-first thousand years C.E. While a few parts of the tantric customs, for example, trademark practices or iconography, extensively originate before the chronicled development of these conventions, the different endeavors to date Tantrism preceding the primary thousand years C.E. depend on an extremely feeble proof.

The tantras themselves, just as related sacred writings (āgama, saṃhitā, and so on), are comprehended by their separate conventions to be uncovered works, at first educated by gods. In the Śaiva convention, sacred texts are accepted to have begun in lessons given by Śiva to his wife, Devī; these lessons were then later passed on to human sages, for example, Matsendranāth. The Śākta and Vaiṣṇava tantric customs, then again, hold the Goddess and Viṣṇu, individually, to be the first divine educator. Some Buddhist tantric customs guarantee that their sacred writings were instructed by enormous ageless buddhas and uncovered to adepts. These legends, while guaranteeing that sacred writings begin in an immortal awesome articulation, in any case, point to their disclosure as being ruminated by extraordinary acknowledged adepts (mahāsiddhas) who lived during the early medieval period, around the seventh through thirteenth hundreds of years, pretty much when most tantric sacred texts became known.

To the degree that tantric sacred texts examine their starting points, these divulgences will, in general, be legendary as opposed to authentic. Regarding these legends as history is normally methodologically unsound. For instance, following the literary model of the Buddhist sūtra kind, various Buddhist tantras start with an opening section (nidāna) that shows the conditions where the sacred text was educated. Various tantras guarantee that they were, similar to the sūtras, at first instructed by Śākyamuni Buddha. Notwithstanding these starting point claims, in any case, there is positively no proof that any of the Buddhist tantras began when the Buddha lived, around the fifth century B.C.E. These sections speak to endeavors to real these functions as stirred discourse (buddhavacana). They cannot be taken as authentic proof.

While endeavors to root parts of tantric conventions in the far off past are theoretical, best-case scenario, there is no uncertainty that these customs, as they rose, were intensely subject to prior Indian conventions of idea and practice. Perhaps the greatest effect on tantric customs was the far more seasoned Vedic convention of Hinduism. Vedic Hinduism highlighted the holy class, Brahmins, who had the sacrosanct obligation to remember the oral holy writing of the custom, the Vedas, and become familiar with the convention's intricate ceremonial practices supported. These ceremonies concentrated on contributions to the divine beings made into a consecrated flame, which ran from to a great extent vegan contributions made into little local (gṛhya) fires that householders were to keep up to the bigger "serious" (śrauta) customs that required creature sacrifice. This convention created around 1500–500 B.C.E., arriving at its pinnacle directly around 500 B.C.E. Only before the ascent of the renunciant customs would challenge it. Even though there was a strain between promoters of the Vedic convention and supporters of a portion of the tantric customs, the tantric conventions drew intensely from Vedic ceremony practice customs regardless.

This getting incorporates a discount adjustment of the key Vedic custom of flame sacrifice, homa, and the change of the Vedic ceremony of regal sanctification, rājyasūya, into the tantric ritual of inception qua "sanctification," abhiṣeka. Indeed, even the particularly tantric routine with regards to picturing oneself as a divinity had Vedic forerunners; some Vedic customs required custom identification with God through internal representation and external ceremonial activities. This was a characteristic result of the Vedic śrauta sacrificial framework's decay around the fifth through thirteenth hundreds of years. Furthermore, its decrease was joined by the parallel ascent of the tantric conventions, which grew new ceremonial frameworks that obtained intensely from Vedic forerunners.

One of the key elements prompting the rise of the tantric conventions was the ascent of the world-revoking śramaṇa development a thousand years sooner around the mid-first thousand years B.C.E. This development, which began inside Hinduism yet prompted the advancement of adversary conventions, to be specific Buddhism and Jainism, was portrayed by its featuring of the objective of freedom (mokṣa) from the cyclic presence (saṃsāra) as the key religious objective, just as the verbalization of unmistakable ways of training for arriving at this objective. These incorporate, most remarkably, renunciation and plainness as a key essential for freedom. Buddhist and Hindu śramaṇa customs held that freedom came about because of a procedure of "enlivening" (bodhi) in which the expert accomplishes a piece of unique information or gnosis (jñāna) that frees one from the cycle of enlivening. The act of contemplation and yoga were viewed as key practices to build up this acknowledgment. Tantric customs acquired this suspicion, and a significant number of the pondering practices, from prior renunciant conventions.

Previously Buddhist tantric conventions acknowledged the cosmological and philosophical structures created by before Buddhist customs, just as a significant number of their reflective practices. Hindu tantric customs, like this, acknowledged and further built up the modern cosmological and mental principles created by the Sāṃkhya school, just as the pensive practices created by its sister Yoga school. Both of these conventions encouraged the transmission of thoughts and practices created by Hindu śramaṇa gatherings.

The early first thousand years C.E. likewise observed another significant advancement in Hinduism, particularly the ascent of the Bhakti reverential development. This improvement happened around a similar time as the ascent of the tantric conventions. It was portrayed by a propensity toward monotheism, in that dedication to a solitary preeminent maker god was viewed as the way to salvation. This inclination is antiquated in Hinduism and is extremely clear in a portion of the later Upaniṣads dating to the second 50% of the principal thousand years B.C.E. Generally early works, for example, the Bhagavad Gīta, assessed to date around 100 C.E., call for commitment to God as the preeminent way to freedom.

The prominence and touchy development of reverential Hinduism significantly affected the tantric conventions. Dedication to God is a focal element of most Hindu tantric conventions, and the Vaiṣṇava Pāñcarātra custom specifically melded both Bhakti and tantric methods of training. Given Buddhism's dismissal of the idea of a preeminent Creator God, one would expect that the Bhakti impact would be less obvious in Buddhist tantric customs. This might be the situation; however, while the impact was less, it was not nonexistent. In the Buddhist setting, commitment is ordinarily constrained to the master, however, this is viewed as a fundamental essential for tantric practice. The need for dedication to the master is emphatically underlined in later works, for example, The Fifty Stanzas on the Guru (Gurupañcāśikā).

The specific time where tantric customs rose in India stays a mystery because of a deficiency of recorded proof in South Asia from the main portion of the primary thousand years C.E. Nonetheless, as we will find in the following segment beneath, the accessible proof proposes that the fifth century C.E. was the no doubt time frame in which the primary tantric customs rose. They likely rose first with regards to the Śaiva convention of Hinduism.

Discover The Chakras (All 7 Chakra)

The Chakras

The tantric texts agree that there is a movement of energy within the human body during sex that can be felt and used. This energy is physical. It rises during the arousal of sex and can be directed and channeled. According to the Hindu tantric texts, we have within us six energy centers known as chakras. These energy centers each have a specific area of human life that they are said to control.

- **The pelvic chakra** — Swadhishthana - is situated at the genitals themselves. This chakra governs our sexual life. A white crescent usually represents it. The mantra for the pelvis chakra is vam.
- **The navel chakra** — Manipuraka — is situated at the navel. This chakra governs our power. A red triangle usually represents it. The mantra for the navel chakra is a ram.
- The heart chakra — Anahata — is situated at the heart. This chakra governs our love. A blue hexagon usually represents it. The mantra for the heart chakra is yam.
- The throat chakra — Vishuddha — is situated at the throat. This chakra governs our communication. A white circle usually represents it. The mantra for the throat chakra is ham.
- The brow chakra — Ajna — is situated between the brows. This chakra governs our intellect and thought processes. An inverted white triangle usually represents it. The mantra for the brow chakra is om.

Each of these chakras also has a Hindu god attributed to it and various symbolic animals, flowers, elements, seasons, and a letter of the Sanskrit alphabet. For a more detailed study of the chakras, see Chakras for Beginners in this series.

The Crown Chakra

Another chakra is worth considering; this is not a true chakra like the others but is known as a shuddha. It is situated at the crown of the head. It is sometimes known as the crown chakra, but it doesn't operate in quite the same way. Its name is Sahasrara, and it is the home of the Goddess Shakti - the God Shiva is said to reside in the brow chakra. The whole point of raising the kundalini energy from the base chakra up the spine to the brow chakra, and then on the crown chakra, is to free Shiva so he may be reunited with Shakti. The great cosmic reunion of the male and female principles can take place. This state of divine bliss is known as samadhi — enlightenment.

Exercise 1

- **For the man**

You should lie down somewhere warm and comfortable. Imagine the site of each chakra as a small, tightly furled flower or small leather bag. As you breathe out, make the mantra sound for each chakra as you visualize it in turn, starting with the base chakra and finishing with the brow chakra. Imagine each chakra as a flower opening as you breathe out - or the small leather bag having drawstrings that are being slowly loosened.

Work your way up to your body, imagining each chakra opening as you make the mantra sound as you exhale. You need to do this exercise with your eyes closed so you can visualize each chakra in turn. This exercise can be done before you make love with your partner to be fully open and ready to feel the energy moving within your body.

- **For the woman**

You should lie down somewhere warm and comfortable. Imagine each chakra as a flower turned upside down. As you breathe out, make the sound of the chakra mantra and imagine each chakra in turn, starting with the base chakra and finishing with the crown chakra, to be the flower slowly turning until it is upright. As it does so, imagine it becoming cooler and stiller as if filled with cold refreshing energy.

You should do this exercise before making love with your partner so that your chakras are open and you are ready to feel the energy moving within your body.

- **Purifying energy**

You can both also do this exercise as a method of cleansing or purifying your energy. As you visualize your energy reaching the crown chakra, imagine it pouring out of the top of your head and being replaced with fresh new energy from your base chakra. Imagine all your past lovers' collected energy being replaced so that you can begin again with a fresh supply.

Exercise 2

Tantric Yoga Relaxation Position

- **Imuladhara Sadhana**

Both you and your lover lie down side by side on your backs but facing opposite ways — your feet to your lover's head and vice versa. The man should lie with the woman along his right side so he can place his right hand lightly across her vulva. The woman can then use her right hand to hold his penis lightly.

This is an exercise to feel the energy rising from the base chakra up through the pelvic chakra and beyond. Try to feel the warmth your lover's hand generates in and through your genitals. As the warmth spreads, focus on it, and feel it spreading upwards as energy.

The man will feel this energy slowly working its way up to his spine, while for the woman, the energy will rise slowly up through her belly first and then her breasts. The man's energy, being hotter and more volatile, may well rise faster, but he should not rush it. The woman's energy, being cooler and slower to arouse, will take longer. If during this exercise, either become aroused to the point of orgasm, then that's all right. Because we are orgasm-oriented in the West, it may take a while to focus on the energy rather than the sexual/spiritual experience. Whatever way you do it, it should be an enjoyable experience. The whole basis of raising the kundalini energy is to share and experience the 'godhead'. If this isn't done in a spirit of delight and enjoyment, it will not be successful. Some have spent a whole lifetime practicing tantric sex and getting nowhere because they do the whole thing as a ritual and completely miss the point.

- **Arousal and Enjoyment**

You have to enter into tantric sex with an approach of delight - what happens is happening, and it's all right. Sometimes there will be a union of the soul with soul and sometimes not - but the journey should be enjoyed without thought of the destination. The experience presented along the way will be lost.

If, during Exercise 2, you become aroused, enjoy it. And there should be no spiritual ego to taunt your partner with: 'Oh, I attained enlightenment and all you achieved was an orgasm.'

Exercise 3

- **Using the Kundalini Energy**

Use the experience as it comes and try to use the energy beneficially. The principal aim or objective of raising the kundalini energy is to reunite or connect with the universe's energy through the unique and wonderful experience of sex. Tantra is a reunion with God.

- **The three forms of energy**

During Exercise 3, the energy may become very sleepy - go with it and use the time given as a meditation. Focus on the brow chakra and allow yourself to appreciate what you can see, feel, and hear. According to the tantric Buddhists, there is a reason why the energy can take any one of many different forms. It may be orgasmic, meditative, or spiritually enlightening - it may even be all three - but the energy generated is being transformed into exactly what you need at any given moment. It may not be what you expect or even what you particularly want, but it will be what you need. The tantric Buddhists recommend that you go with it; if you don't fight the universe, it will provide you with everything you need.

- **Being in touch with your body**

Exercise 3 will put you in touch with your genital feelings. We focus on our genitals, usually only in the rush of orgasm or being caressed. During this exercise, you can focus on both yours and your partner's genitals. How do they feel? Wholesome and healthy? Or is there some residue guilt or inhibition there? According to the tantric Buddhists, we sometimes fail to achieve a truly deep spiritual/sexual experience because we are somehow hanging on to our fears and repression. During Exercise 3, you can explore your feelings about your sexuality - and your body as a sexual instrument.

History Of Tantra

The original tantra, also called "red" or "left hand," is linked to ancient matriarchal societies and has female energy as its center. While the Tantra called "White" or "right-handed," created later due to Muslim infiltrations, derives from Indian patriarchal societies.

The difference between Red Tantra and White Tantra is radical. The second, White Tantra, is based on static and solitary meditations. At the same time, Red Tantra is a practice in which meditation is not just immobility and seriousness. In Red Tantra, meditation and sacredness are experienced in every moment of existence, through deep listening and attention to what is happening in us and outside of us. Meditation occurs while dancing, working, embracing, eating, drinking, playing, and talking.

There is a lot of confusion about what Tantra is and, above all, a lot of targeted misinformation due to the persecutions to which the Original Tantra was subjected. Tantra carries the burden of false commonplaces, such as that of free sex. Unlike other disciplines that have been less polluted, Tantra is for many a kind of Yoga practice; for others, an orgiastic practice and for still others a religion.

The Origin of Tantra

According to the almost unanimous opinion of scholars, the archaic nature of Red Tantra dates back to pre-Vedic cultures, to the very beginnings of Indian history, identifiable with the Harappei, Sindhu, and other Dravidian populations which developed their civilization in the Indus valley. According to some, in the third millennium BC, these populations were widespread in a huge territory from Spain to the Ganges valley. Their precursors had settled in the Indus valley in Mehrgar, starting from 7000 BC, and their traces can be found up to 5500 BC.

Dravidian populations, therefore, appeared there around 6000-5000 BC, had their apogee between 2300 and 1300 BC., and disappeared, rather quickly, in 100 years between 1900 and 1800 B.C. The disappearance's reasons were attributed in the past to invasions of the Arii population from the north. Today there is a tendency to attribute it to a tectonic movement that caused the Aravali hills in northern Rajastan to rise, depriving the river that supported the Dravida civilization (the Ghaggar-Hakra) of most of its tributaries.

The Harappei population showed a marked interest in the arts and well-being. Theirs was a matriarchal society, the most important central monument of their city, it was a large swimming pool; the element of water was fundamental in their society, and there has already been a bathroom in every home. The woman was at the center of culture, focused on the mother goddess. The female figure dominated the sanctuaries and, with open arms and legs, offered herself to adoration. The Harappei used to keep a large bed in the center of the most important room in the house and practiced Tantra. Their religion was closely connected with the body, well-being, and sexuality.

It can be said that Red Tantra is the expression of all those practices, which also include sexuality. Red Tantra includes practices carried out in groups, including contact and "vehiculation" through the senses.

In the centuries following Tantra's birth, in India, due to the Islamic invasions, the original Red Tantra was officially suppressed and forced to transform itself into an occult school. Today we know it as Tantra Yoga. It has completely lost its peculiarity of a concrete approach to sexuality, typical of the original Tantra.

In practice, the White Tantra is a Red Tantra but censored by all those practices that moralists could understand as unbecoming. Today the White Tantra, which is a mystification of the original Tantra, is used in the West for commercial purposes. Almost all Tantra schools practice White Tantra and therefore do not teach Tantra.

True Tantra is the Way of reconnection with one's Self. It is the Way; that of discovering our genotypic sexual energies that are manifested through the knowledge and practice of the Original Tantra.

The Tantra texts

The Tantras are a series of texts of Central Asian origin (India, Kashmir, Bengal, Orissa, Assam, Kerala, Indus Valley, etc.) like the collections of the Puranas or the Vedas, but which manifest themselves in the manner of esoteric texts divine revealed and are often written as if they were the gods Shiva and Shakty (and their emanations) in-person speaking and are part of the Hindu texts Agama.

The origin of the Tantras is pre-Vedic, which is much older than the texts on which Hinduism and the Vedas are based, and originates from the ancient matriarchal peoples and, in general, all the collections of Hindu texts are deeply influenced by the Tantra. No Hindu and Brahmin ritual does not have its roots in Tantra.

The Tantras were transcribed long after their birth. Previously, the tradition was handed down only orally from master to teacher, from teacher to teacher. In fact, in Tantra, unlike Hinduism, the teachers could be men or women. Starting from about the VI AD instead, the written transcriptions of many Tantras begin to appear.

Tantric texts have more than one reading and can be experienced at different levels of intuition. According to the Tantric tradition, a text can confuse or illuminate. Tantric texts often speak by aphorisms (sutra and karika) and often generate immense commentaries that explain aphorisms that can sometimes be difficult to understand.

The term Tantra, linked to the ancient texts, was then translated to indicate the Spiritual Experiential Way that follows these ancient teachings.

More than 500 existing Tantras are known which belong to different initiatory ways or lineages (Aghora, Ālvār, Bāul, Gauḍīya, Kālāmukha, Pāśupata, Sahajiyā, Śaivasiddhānta, Saura, Shakta, Spanda, Surya, Śrīvidyā, Trika, Kālīkula, Kānpaṭha, Kāpālika, Krama, Kaula, Lākula, Liṅgāyat, Nātha, Nāyaṇar, Pāñcarātra, etc.). Many of them have never even been translated from Sanskrit. Other tantric texts have been lost, and it is not known what they handed down. It is said that the texts reached a considerable number of 14000 volumes. So the panorama of tantric initiatory texts is very vast, and not all Tantras treat themes equally according to the lineage to which they belong. So this also generates some confusion regarding the teachings. Some Tantric Texts can be of a few pages, others of thousands of pages.

It should therefore be understood that different teachings are grouped under the word Tantra. However, on many points, many Tantra essentially agrees. It cannot be said that the various tantric texts contradict each other, but that they simply give certain importance more to one aspect than to another. Some Tantras favor the transmission of the concept of Presence, others of the body's concept, others concerning Sexuality. A generally shared aspect is the "freed in life," that is, the unnecessary need for countless reincarnations to dissolve Karma. In fact, in tantra, it is indicated that by following certain rituals or teachings, it is possible to dissolve the karmic knots quickly, soon arriving at a knowledge of oneself also through the experimentation of eros and sexuality in the encounter between Shiva and Shakti and in any case following a way away from the renunciation of the body.

The revelations of the Tantras are considered superior to the Vedas because they are much more effective in the liberation of men and lead them faster to a higher stage and are more suitable for the current cosmic era, the Kaliyuga. Tantra considers the Vedic texts valid, but on a lower level as basic general rules, but are then integrated by higher and esoteric specific tantric teachings.

Tantric texts do not address the renunciation ascetic of the world. Still, on the contrary, they address those who live in the world, together with others, without going away or dedicating themselves to asceticism.

How did Tantra Arrive in the West

In conjunction with the sexual liberation of the 60s and 70s and the emancipation of women, some scholars and philosophers began to talk about Tantra and trying to make it a practicable approach even in the West, made the rituals more agile and less blocking in the calculation of breath and holding of positions. Currently, emancipation allows women to get closer to the sexual world. However, in western society, it is still believed that sex is more masculine than feminine. Cultural heritage does not allow women to focus on that.

In the West today, Tantra aims to draw two maps that indicate how to make the sexual experience spiritual and unite the earth with the sky, in a terrain where separation and judgment vanish. A world, the western one, where there are no schools and traditions, and everything is to be invented and experimented with. In the West, the sexual sphere has been a world crushed for two millennia by taboos and religions, which often finds its only expression in private clubs or porn sites.

Tantra and the Way of Liberation

With all its erotic experiences, Tantra is nothing more than a tool that opens up internal physical, emotional, and energetic spaces and opens up to awareness. Tantra is, therefore, only Red Tantra. It is the way of liberation that opens up to the true expression of oneself, and that allows one to exit, both in the imaginary and in the real, from the dimension of the matrix in which sexual energy is mechanically channeled for improper purposes.

Sex and sexual energy are very different things. The idea of sex is what in the imagination has settled during education, stories, and commercial pornography, a program, therefore, but so rooted that individuals believe that it is precisely that pre-programmed way that sexual energy must be expressed. A program that is then gradually enhanced with the repetitive experiences that add up as memories.

The vital energy or commonly known as sexual energy (Kundalini), is instead what is the essence of the man at its origin; it is what we carry in our genes, but due to the education received in the matrix, is then unnaturally expressed in the facts.

Over time, with the help of religious morality, the matrix selected a sexual modality aimed entirely at procreation, therefore mechanical and centered on penetration and orgasm intended as a goal to be achieved; as if all the wonder of the contact between the bodies should be enclosed in the act of a few minutes, between the two genital organs. Many people believe they are sexually free because they do a lot of that mechanical sex. In reality, they are just more slaves; slaves to a trap where true sexual energy is humiliated and crushed.

Tantric Sex Basics

When you begin to follow the path of tantric sex, you begin to find a change in yourself. You find yourself changing how you view yourself and how you view the world. You find yourself looking at relationships that will last a lifetime. Through your journey, you will learn that every man and woman has a certain divinity level in them. You will start to view sex as a sacred act instead of just a physical act. You will also learn to love deeper and find that you are soaring to different levels of bliss.

You will only have a successful journey when you relieve yourself from any preconceived notions. You should not think of what you need to do and what your lover must do to please you. When you read this, you will learn to identify new ideas about yourself and embrace new ideas. You will also find out how to have great sex!

You will learn the basic concepts of tantric sex and identify new exciting ways to live and love.

The Yin And The Yang – Which Is Male, and Which Is Female?

You must be familiar with the stereotypes that men are from Mars and women are from Venus. This implies that men are assertive and extremely powerful. At the same time, women are soft and fragile who are only fit for nurturing. There are other stereotypes that men do not show any feelings whatsoever. At the same time, women have a plethora of emotion ready to unleash itself in a second. It has also been said that women do not take credit for their work, since being outgoing is something only men are familiar with. With years passing by, the way men and women think has drastically changed.

Tantric sex is a firm follower of the fact that men and women do have opposite characteristics. This is the elementary principle of the Tantra. The eastern theories claim that the Yin represents feminism while the Yang represents masculinity. But there is no concrete proof that a woman cannot have Yang characteristics or that a man cannot have Yin characteristics. Rather than viewing men and woman as two entities, you should begin to focus on the energies. The Tantra believes in the amalgamation of these two energies.

Shiva and Shakti

The most common image of the Yin and the Yang is the Hindu divine couple Lord Shiva and Goddess Shakti. Lord Shiva represents the entire universe since he is considered the creator and Goddess Shakti represents the root of all energy. The union of the two deities creates a longing in you and every other human being treated like a god or a goddess. You will learn to worship your partner as a god or a goddess.

The male energy found in Lord Shiva represents ecstasy while the energy in Goddess Shakti represents wisdom. This magical combination is what helps a person attain enlightenment. This perfect couple is always represented in numerous entwined positions – either dancing or embracing or standing together. There are other positions where Goddess Shakti is wrapped around Lord Shiva with her legs propped around his hips. The dancing position by far is the most sacred since they can free their spirit, giving them a chance to attain enlightenment.

Understanding the Opposites

You may have made divisions amongst you and your partner. You have first to recognize and understand these divisions to strike a balance between the opposite energies. There are quite a few stereotypical characteristics that you may relate to. You will have to identify those characteristics and make note of them. You have to go from one extreme. You should ask your partner to do this too. You will then have to see how you can embrace the extreme characteristics you and your partner have. You have to identify how you can strike a balance between the polarities that exist between you and your partner. You will have to identify the Yin to your partner's Yang and vice versa.

You might now wonder if it is true that opposites attract. Sit back and think for yourself. You will be able to respond to the question on your own correctly. Try analyzing your past relationships. See how you and your partner were different from each other. Identify whether the differences were complemented by each other. This will help you analyze your future relationships as well.

My Partner Is My Beloved

Tantra is not mad love but sacred love. You are honoring your partner and cherishing your partner while making love. You will shower unconditional love on your partner. When you speak with your partner, use loving words like 'darling' or 'beloved'. You will find that those little words have aroused feelings of love within your partner. Call your partner with the aforementioned loving words when talking about him or her in public. You might find it strange to do so, but you will be sending out a message of love to your speaking person.

The Desire Spectrum

You will find yourself with new views of desire. You may feel a desire every time you think of someone. You may comment on how you want a guy or how hot a girl is when you see them passing. You only feel these desires when you feel incomplete. Since you feel incomplete, you always want another person. You find yourself feeling needy and feeling wanted. But when you do get the person you want; you begin to want something more. You want someone prettier, more interesting and sometimes someone richer. Through tantric sex, you will be able to detach yourself from superficial needs. This will help you create a healthier relationship with your partner.

You Feel Invested To Say What You Want!

When you find yourself empowered, you can set boundaries both during sex and in life in general. You find yourself with a new level of self — esteem. In tantric sex, you OWN your body and your soul. When your partner wants you to enter you, he must ask for your permission. You should not be afraid and have to say yes or no as the situation demands. You have to stop and say that you do not want to be touched in a way that is not comfortable. You empower your partner when you speak the truth this way. You will be giving your partner the methods to use to please you. You have to be okay with how you are touched and how you feel.

Tantric Meditation

Tantric meditation is an active and fundamental part of tantric thought, at the center of which is the manifest of the universe, created as a physical and sensorial expression of the un-manifest. It is through immersion in the former that full unity with the latter becomes possible. This however entails a rigid discipline, variable according to the practitioner's level of consciousness. However, each level has its common denominator the work on the harmonization of male and female energy, Shiva and Shakty, which are also close to the Taoist concepts of Yin and Yang. This activity aims to properly awaken and channel Kundalini energy, the custodian of the secret of enlightenment. Tantric philosophy has roots both in archaic Buddhism and Hinduism. Still, it is believed that Hinduism inherited the tantra from Buddhism, and not vice versa, since the oldest Tantra (philosophical reference texts) are of Buddhist compilation and date back to 350 AD. Today, tantric meditation and more generally tantrism are known in the chronicles as techniques to improve sexual performance or to intervene in difficult situations as a couple. Most of what is said about it is limiting, if not completely wrong.

Basic tantric meditation helps the practitioner find peace and balance, as it manages to connect each phase, which remains disconnected from the others during everyday life. Integration occurs because, during tantra practice, emotions and different attitudes are combined, with harmony. In addition to this, given the structuring and repetitiveness of tantra practice, this type of meditation can be effective as a stabilizing factor in a society characterized by being destabilizing. Meditation thus helps to make life flow in an interrupted flow of continuity. The tantric approach helps alleviate the couple's tensions about the sexual dimension of the practice, bringing benefits in case of frigidity, premature ejaculation, and even impotence, when this has psychological roots.

Methods of Tantric Mediation

The different teachings of the masters, which have followed one another over the centuries, use very similar techniques, having a solid common basis. The extinction of the samskaras, the accumulated karmic seeds that prevent the expansion of consciousness. An example of a meditative process that is based on Tantric tradition is the one proposed below:

- **Iiswara Pranidhana** — the practitioner, through different stages, develops awareness of his deep spiritual nature. In this first stage, the conditionings of the mind and the karma of past lives are slowly removed

- **Madhu vidya** — the practitioner introduces meditation into daily life

- **Tattva dharana** — through the use of meditative tools, such as mantra and yantra, the practitioner begins the deep purification of the subtle elements, dissolving the nodes in the nadis (channels through which, in traditional Indian medicine and spiritual knowledge, the energies such as prana of the physical body, the subtle body, and the causal body are said to flow) and raising the level of the kundalini

- **Pranayama** – through a breathing technique typical of yoga, the yogi controls his vital energy, placing it at the service of the development of consciousness

- **Shodana** – a system of deep purification and empowerment of the potentials of the subtle centers of the body is developed

- **Dhyana** – this phase of meditation leads the practitioner to abandon the meditative supports used to merge with his half.

You can also start meditating with simpler techniques, which can be learned during a course that is not limited to asanas only.

Tantric or tantra meditation can also be used in a couple's relationship, not necessarily with therapeutic intent, but also as a way of knowing the other. Unlike what can be expected, tantra is not a sex guide, but a spiritual path that can also be done in a couple whose goal is awareness. There is no precise starting point. A precise arrival point is not described, but paths are identified that do not necessarily have to do with sexual intercourse, aiming to unlock the energies. Men and women are carriers of complementary and different energy flows that can "blossom" thanks to common meditation. Sexologists can use these techniques to improve the couple's affinity and knowledge before tackling any problems immediately on a physical level.

Mantra Meditation

For "formal" meditation with mantras, adopt a sitting posture. For casual practice, you can repeat the mantra in the back of your mind, with your eyes open, during other daily doings.

Singing the mantra energizes you quickly. Scanning it with a certain cadence calms the mind. If your repetition is too fast or too slow, it will become an automatic process and your mind will wander too much or fall prey to sleep.

The rapidity with which the mantra is spelled out also varies according to the length of the mantra: short ones (from one to three syllables) are often reiterated more slowly than long mantras.

Since the speed varies according to the technique you are adopting, the advice is to experiment with different repetition speeds and determine which one is the most effective. It is better to maintain a uniform repetition rate rather than changing it several times during practice.

Suppose your mind is very active and full of thoughts. In that case, it may be useful to "increase the volume" in repeating the mantra, making it stronger and more incisive. If your mind is quieter, on the other hand, the mantra can become more subtle and be recited in a low voice, like a high-frequency sound that can barely be heard. The word itself is almost gone and the mantra is perceived more as sound vibrations than as a punctuated phrase.

You may or may not be capable to sync the mantra with your breath. Some options to do it better are:

- Inhale and exhale as you say the mantra. If the mantra is very small, like om, you can repeat it one time while inhaling, and one more while exhaling. You can also increase your speed and repeat it three times for each inhalation and three times for exhalation. If the mantra is lengthy, then you can recite half of it during inspiration and the second half while exhaling.

- Exhale. Inhale without reciting the mantra, and spell out the mantra only on exhalation.

Just focus on the mantra, paying attention to breathing. With time, the breath tends to synchronize naturally with the rhythm of the mantra.

Progressing on Mantra Meditation

The more we reiterate our mantra, the more we give it energy. A one-syllable mantra, it is thought that after 125,000 reiterations "gets its own life". It is our repetitive attention that works with the mantra and loads it. The mantra then gets to be the strongest thought in your mind, and then you can count on it to give you peace and concentration in your life.

Once the mantra gets this momentum, repetition becomes easier. It is as if once we manage to "start" or "access" the mantra then it goes on by itself, bringing us into a state of internal silence.

The following is the typical progress of the practice:

- **Verbal acting** — repeat it aloud. This simple mechanism involves your senses, facilitating in keeping your attention focused.

- **The whisper** — the mouths and the tongue move, but only produce a faint sound. This part is more subtle and profound than verbal acting.

- **Mental recitation** — reiterate the mantra only in your mind. At the beginning, of course, there will be some action in the tongue and throat, but over time they too will stop, and the exercise will be entirely in the mind. This stage is the most common in mantra meditation.

- **Spontaneous listening** — at this stage you are no longer reiterating the mantra. Still, the mantra continues naturally alone in your mind. No need to worry about the intensity and speed. Just pay attention to the Mantra repeating it as it naturally wants to be reiterated. This stage is referred as ajapa japa.

There is a slow but significant progression from the first to the last level. A very common mistake in beginners is to skip stages and go directly to the mental stage, or spontaneous repetition. Although it is impossible to get there immediately, it is much easier to follow this scale to master meditation with mantras.

Even if you dislike verbal acting and want to jump straight to the mental level, I recommend that you do at least a few cycles of acting whispered at the beginning. This will help you focus your brain on the mantra.

Wherever you are on this progression if you find out that your mind is disengaging from the mantra, distracted by other thoughts, or sleepy, stop for a few seconds and then employ a more conscious action in repeating the mantra, until you come to an effective result.

Yantra Meditation

As explained earlier, Yantras are geometric designs conceived as containers of spiritual energies. In the Himalayan region of northern India, where traces of their use were found in 2000 BC, they are still used today to cultivate the universal properties of devotion and purification, for the spirit. The practice originates from the "mantras" (vibration of sounds) and the yantra are the visual representation of the vibrations and are part of Tantra's philosophical practice.

If you are interested in deepening meditation, but you are not comfortable with the traditional method of sitting in silence or experimenting with a different technique, the creation of yantra can be for you. The yantra images are the symbol of your research. Studying the trait, the shape, the color, becoming aware of the time, and the realization's devotion are the ingredients for realizing the inner beauty. You will be surprised by the power of the creative force that emanates. The power of work through these symbols continues to manifest itself even after unconscious creation within you. The yantra can be taken with you, at home, in the office, and remain a foothold for a calm and positive energy recharge. Specific effects of the practice depend on the type of design you choose to work with.

Now you can choose a shape or shapes which to some extent are in greater resonance with you. Or even better, redesign them by comparing yourself with the process, patience, observation, and attention required. Or make a color copy and internalize it by meditating on it. If you intend to color it, use pastels, start from the top and continue clockwise, from the outside until you get to the bindu, the point in the center. Working in this direction, you visualize the internalization process, which symbolically proceeds "from the outside of the mind" towards a spiral movement that takes you inside the immutable part of the self. Each color has been chosen to emit frequencies that resonate within the shape, so it is advisable to stay within the chosen color scheme. For example, the passion yantra must always be red but feel free to choose the red tone you like best. Coloring is an important part of the meditation process, live it with awareness.

Benefits of Tantric Sex

Tantric sex has a myriad of different benefits, and here, we'll highlight and discuss in detail some of the benefits tantric sex has to offer.

Rejuvenates Your Sexual Health

Tantric sex is wonderful for sexual health, especially for women, but men do as well.

When you have a lot of orgasms frequently in your brain, it stimulates brain waves, and the chemistry you have will alter.

For many people, sex is used as a way to relax, but it's more than just a simple ejaculation or climax. It's a way to help release those energies which are tied up.

Think about your current sexual health. Do you orgasm a lot? Do you sometimes have sex without being fully aroused or even an orgasm? Sometimes this happens, especially with women. Some women take much longer to get aroused or even to experience orgasms, which means that for them, sex is more than an activity they do to benefit their partner rather than themselves.

But, when you use tantric sex, the idea is to benefit both parties, not just the guy who is having sex but also the woman. That means, you'll both have amazing orgasms, and you'll feel better about sex as well. You'll want to have sex more, and sex will be better, more meaningful for you.

That can do several great things for both your physical and mental health and we'll discuss that here.

Depression and Stress Relief

Depression and stress are the biggest mental hurdles that we have in our world today. However, sex is a way to help relieve it. But, if you're just having quickie after quickie, without really having a deeper, more immersive connection with your partner, can you say that it's stress-relieving?

Chances are, it's not. You need to have that long, relaxing sexual experience to be happier. While five hours might be excessive, it's significantly more than the five minutes they were having beforehand for some people.

Tantric sex helps with stress and depression, and it can help you feel better too. When you orgasm, a lot of the stress you experience while having sex magically melts away, resulting in you being happier, and much healthier too.

It can even affect the brain chemistry too, probably in ways you've already experienced. Still, they're worth mentioning regardless, for example, the endocrine glands start to increase, meaning a much higher high, some serotonin excreted, some DHEA, and testosterone too, which will affect your physical wellness too. All of this is there, and there are even some studies that say when you have more orgasms, you'll experience greater mental health and wellness.

Sex isn't just a temporary orgasm and temporary happiness either. With tantric sex, it takes it to the next level, ups the ante a little bit. When you experience tantric sex, you're experiencing a more intimate and personal connection with the person you love, and that in turn can make you feel utterly amazing.

Tantric sex is a good thing to have, and it's something that, with the way things are sometimes, can help you mentally feel good.

Depends On the Bond

How many times do you have sex with your partner, and it feels almost...forgettable? Sex shouldn't be some forgettable experience. Some of us have sex for our partners' sake, and sometimes, we just have sex to have sex.

But with tantric sex, it changes the game. With tantric sex, you're using that connection you've got with the other person, and in turn, building more understanding with the other person, and some wellness and happiness too. You will feel more in-tune with your partner, and much happier as well you'll feel the connection grow between the two of you.

And it isn't just a physical connection, it's a mental connection too. If you sometimes feel the distance between you and your partner, having tantric sex will help you enjoy the moment, enjoy your partner, and make things better between the two of you. So yes, it will help develop a healthier connection and a deeper understanding.

Physical Benefits

Orgasms do possess a physical benefit too. They can improve your health a lot. It can help make your body stronger through cardiovascular health, endocrine, immune function, and nervous system health. Suppose you have tantric sex at least twice a week. In that case, it releases an antibody called immunoglobulin A, or IgA, which protects your body from illness.

Orgasms also can help alleviate depression, and help you feel and look younger. Some also believe it'll make your lifespan stronger, strengthen your immune system, and improve your overall health. However, there are still studies that need to be done to verify these results completely.

But, sexual experience and exposure to semen do help boost the moods I most women. In many cases, it can help with your mood enhancements, your emotional bands, and ultimate intimacy too. Both males and females can get benefits from this too. This isn't just one or the other but having sex together will provide these benefits since it'll be an activity both of you participate in too.

There is also the fact that it can be a wonderful cardio for the body. Sex burns a lot of calories, and orgasm does too. That's why you must consider this since even making love requires energy, and if you're going for a long time, it can be a wonderful workout.

It also naturally relaxes the body. Tantric sex, in particular, does it, since you're calming both the body and the mind down to be in-sync with your partner. That mutual togetherness alone stimulates your vagus nerve, thereby relaxing the body and promoting wellness too. Over time, you'll start to feel the muscles that were stretched start to relax, and you'll practice diaphragmic breathing too.

Tantric sex is great for the physical body, and it is a good thing to do for you, not just because it feels great, but because it makes you feel great too.

A Woman's Orgasm

Tantric sex, in particular, will help with a woman's orgasm. There is a big difference between the ordinary orgasm that you get from sex and tantric orgasms. Often, it will change how the woman feels.

These can often last for hours, and in women, this can change their sexual health. There is a command during a tantric orgasm that reaches your brains' control center, and hat's through the hypothalamus and the pituitary gland. I will majorly benefit the sex life of women.

A lot of the hormone oxytocin gets released during a tantric orgasm. This alone can boost your mood, the position you feel in life, passion, emotion, and social skills. Having tantric sex can do all of this, and I can benefit you in your daily activities.

It Will Make You More Patient

Tantric sex isn't just for sexual pleasure, it helps with developing life skills and building on weaknesses.

Do you sometimes kind of just want to get it done rather than go through the deep connection at the moment? You might not even realize it because hormones fuel your body and mind. Still, tantric sex promotes patience, which is something of a virtue that everyone can have during sex. However, this can also help you to build a more in-depth, better connection with your partner.

Sometimes, tantric sex is a little bit awkward, since many people aren't used to just sitting there, focusing on their partner, breathing together, and developing a real look at the person they're with. Some people don't even realize they do this either.

Do you tend to have sex with either your eyes closed or the lights off? While dimming the lights aids to the ambiance, tantric sex makes it a little different. Tantric sex is a meditative process, and they encourage you to hold back the orgasm. It didn't denial, it's your conscious effort to hold it back so you and your partner can have a mindful moment together.

Patience develops naturally from this. You might not even grasp it, but you learn to understand and appreciate your partner a whole lot more after engaging in tantric sex. Those things that used to annoy now and then? Well now, if you practice tantric sex, this patience develops, and you grow stranger with your partner over time.

Helps with Problem Solving

This might give you the impression that it is strange, but for those starting, it is a different type of activity that you might not be used to. Those who are beginners or new to the experience might realize that the positions required for tantric sex are much more varied than just the same old places.

Some of them might not even provide much pleasure to you either.

This requires you to work together with your partner. It has sex a team activity, where both of you need to talk it out and work together as well, in order to enjoy pleasure.

This can oftentimes be embarrassing because both of you are vulnerable in this state, but it helps with problem-solving skills and builds that connection. Plus, if you're a team, you'll have a much healthier relationship outside of the bedroom, and work to solve the problems you have going on outside of the bedroom as well.

This also stimulates creativity. That's because we're embracing the concept of "supra sexuality" which expresses our purpose which is creativity and empowerment to unlock our full potential. Sex might be used to create human life of course, but it also brings forth new and creative actions that will help you experience a pleasurable sensation to achieve the goals that you have during intercourse as well.

Let's You Be Selfless

Are there times that you feel like your partner is a little selfish in the bedroom? Do you sometimes think you might be a tiny bit selfish? It might be because you're not withholding your orgasm.

There is a great benefit in doing this, and that's something to mention. Often, people don't realize that tantric sex offers the power of liberation, which allows you to have a fantastic experience that is often compared to glimpsing into the other person's cosmic consciousness, fostering a deeper, more responsible understanding of the person.

Often, some people don't realize how selfish they are until they have the tantric orgasm, changing their lives and blowing their minds. Often, they might not even realize that they are like this until it happens.

But for the other person, it can benefit them too. Sex is a two-person activity. If you and your partner are both not talking out what will benefit the other person, and your partner isn't a little bit selfless, it can cause problems later. You need to walk into this with the idea of supporting one another into orgasms since this will help others remember and get a better idea of giving rather than just receiving.

We're a culture focused on the receiving end of sex. While it's fun, also giving to the other person can have some marked benefit to you as well.

Tantric Sex in the Relationship and General Tips

Note that tantra goes beyond sex — you can work or choose not to go to that at the very least. You and your partner can use tantric values to build up other activities.

Foreplay

This can be anything you want—oral, a massage, a shower together. Ensure you and your partner is present whatever you do.

Sit before your friend. Look into the eyes of each other. Start to move your bodies while you breathe slowly.

After five minutes, begin to sensually touch each other and massage one another's arms, legs, neck, and other parts.

After five more minutes, start kissing — and just kissing. Concentrate on every physical sensation you feel right now.

Sex (optional!)

You may or may not build-up to sex! Tantra is more related than anything.

If you're sexy, move slowly. And don't be scared of being imaginative! Try new places, touch each other in new ways, and explore unknown desires.

But above all, plunge deep into the experience, allowing the sensation to develop as you spend time in one sensual exercise before moving to the next.

Cuddling or Laying Together

Lying with your partner helps you to share, weave, and link energy.

Find a spooning place to do this. The rear partner sends power (giver), while the front partner consumes it (receiver).

Next together, connected with your chest and stomachs, the donor must wrap his arms around the sender, his hand over the heart of the recipient. The receiver should rest on top of it.

Lie a few moments away, and then begin to harmonize your breath and allow your power to flow freely.

- **Let's build intensity.** Gaze in the eyes of each other as long as possible without blinking.
- **Sync the breathing.** You can attempt to inhale and exhale together or inhale as your partner exhales.

- **Ask what your partner wants.** Call out what you enjoy when they touch and play with you, and ask them to continue. Do the same for your partner.
- **Set your training goal.** Whether your relationship is better or strengthened, you and your partner should participate in the session, knowing what you both want.

General Tips and Tricks on Tantric Sex

Stock is not one-size-fit-to-all in Pinterest Tantra. There are a few things you can do to enhance your training and make it a rewarding and enjoyable experience: • It is possible to be naked. You can start dressing and remain dressed, or you can cut every inch of fabric. The trick is to do anything that makes you feel relaxed. It is up to you whether that means to be nude or not.

- **Be careful about your breath.** A vital part of tantra is deep breathing. By concentrating on your breath, you can be present at the moment and immerse yourself in the experience.
- **Involve all your senses.** Light a few fragrant candles. Sing a little sensual, soft music. Slowly touch yourself or your friend. Stare in the eyes of each other. Enjoy the taste of the kisses of your friend. Engaging all your senses during your tantra will help you feel more deeply each pleasurable feeling.
- **Go slow.** Go slow. An important part of tantra is to learn to think and experience it all deeper. And this is the way to go slowly. Don't hurry tantra; instead, relax and enjoy the practice every second.
- **Discover the whole body of your partner.** Slowly drive your hands over the body of your friend. Let them explore your mouth with their tongue when kissing. Or move your lips up and down your neck softly. Make them the same.

- **Experiment.** Experiment. For example, Kink and BDSM also integrate tantric concepts. So you don't have to adhere to tradition when you practice tantra. Think outside the box — and have fun with it if that means using a container.
- **You do not need to do full tantra.** In what you already do in the bedroom, you can add elements-either alone or with your partner. This could include relaxation in the foreplay or concentrate more on deep breathing during a solo session.

The Most Effective Method to Synchronize Your Breath

Your breath is fundamental to any tantric practice. Breathing enables you to free your brain, interface with your body, and feel each sensation all the more completely. At the point when you practice any of these methods, make sure to sit upright and in an agreeable position consistently.

The Stimulating Breath

This strategy can help raise vitality and increment mindfulness.

To do this:

1. Close your eyes and mellow your tummy.

2. Inhale and breathe out rapidly through your nose, keeping your mouth shut.

3. Try three in-and-out breaths every second for 15 seconds.

4. Breathe typically after the cycle closes, at that point, attempt again for 20 seconds, expanding by five seconds until you arrive at one entire moment.

The 4-7-8 Breath

This strategy can assist you with discharging strain and loosen up your body. You can attempt this procedure while sitting opposite your accomplice, synchronizing your breath.

To do this:

1. Exhale through your mouth, at that point, close your mouth.
2. Inhale discreetly through your nose to a psychological tally of four.
3. Hold the breath for a check of seven.
4. Exhale through your mouth totally to a check of eight.
5. Repeat the cycle on three additional occasions for a sum of four breaths.

The Counting Breath

This is another type of contemplation that enables you to clear your psyche, locate your inside, and interface with your body.

To do this:

1. Shut your eyes and take a couple of full breaths.
2. Let your breath stream normally.
3. Inhale; at that point, check "one" to yourself as you breathe out.
4. On the following, breathe out, check "two." Work your way up to "five."
5. Repeat the cycle, beginning at "one" and completing on "five."
6. Don't go past "five," generally, your psyche and consideration will start to meander.
7. Try tallying your breath for 10 minutes.

Tantric Massage

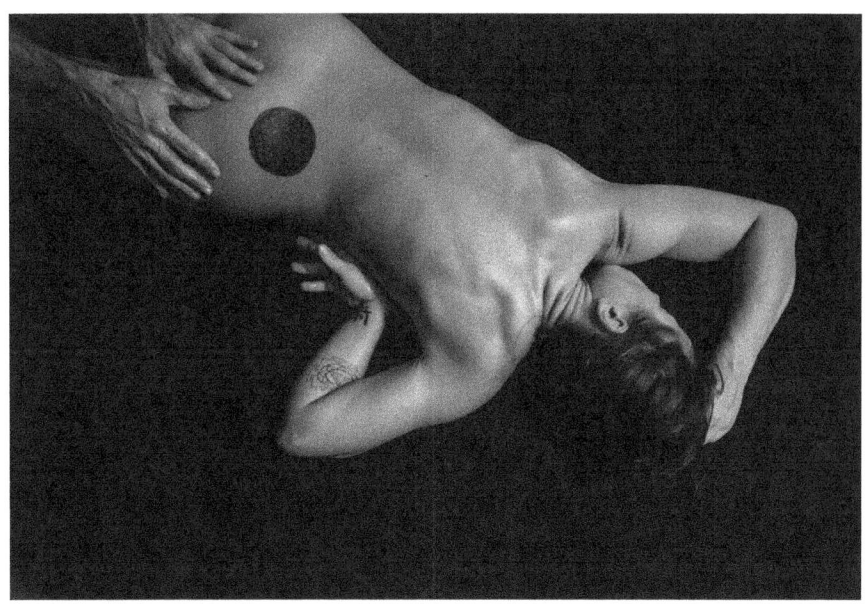

Massages are one of the best ways to rid the body of tension, spread healing energies, improve your blood circulation, and when it comes to tantra, they can help to arouse your lover sexually. Massages are one of the best ways to help sexual partners show extra intimacy.

By nature, humans crave touch, and a massage is a natural and easy way to get that much-needed touch. So how can you do this? First off, you don't have to go out and get a special certificate or training to perform tantric massages. What you do need is to have a yearning and intention to genuinely satisfy your partner through the intricate capacities of your hands.

What Is Tantric Massage?

Before we dive into the actual massage techniques, we need to go over what tantric massage actual is, how it is different from other massages, and the main benefits that come with it. The tantric massage that we know today was created from several different sources, which are mainly a combination of tantric philosophy and influences from important Western thinkers.

The main features of a tantric massage are:

- A spiritual awakening is the ultimate and true goal of tantra and tantric massage.
- Clothes should never be worn during the massage, so private parts will, most of the time, be exposed.
- To heighten or boost orgasmic or sexual experiences.
- To remove blockages in different areas of your spirit, mind, body, and consciousness.
- Tantric massage focuses on the usage and potential of your sexual energy so that it benefits you and doesn't limit you.

Benefits

Just like any other type of massage, the tantric way has several different benefits, as well as a couple of extra benefits that make tantra a little more special. The main inherent benefits of a massage are:

- Relief from stress, anxiety, and pain
- Improved immunity and health
- Improved mood

- Increased wellbeing

Some benefits that are added with the massage being tantric are:

- Higher spiritual awareness
- More intense sexual experiences
- Improved sex drive and libido

With that being said, let's look at some techniques and tips to help you get started with your tantric massages.

Getting Ready

For those who have never experienced it, the thought of a tantric massage is oftentimes very intriguing, if not completely intimidating. Some even view it as taboo, which is a very unfortunate byproduct of our culture today.

On the other hand, people who know what tantric massage is, see it as a unique, irreplaceable, and an exciting practice that can do a lot for a person and their partner's wellbeing. Since the majority of people don't understand what it is and how exactly it works, they don't even think it's an option for them to use in their lives.

To have the best tantric massaging session, you will want you and your partner to take turns massaging one another. This form of massage will require the receiver to be completely open and receptive and to be willing to surrender themself completely to the experience.

To help get things started, the following are some preparations you need to make before you get started:

- **Prepare the Space**

You will want to get the space you are going to use ready for the massage. This could be your bedroom, living room, or any other private space. Make sure you have comfortable bedding and soft pillows. You can also place several light candles around the room, and you can also use scent candles to aid in the ambiance. Make sure that they are placed far away from anything flammable. Turn off or dim your regular lights.

You should also have a glass of water or wine nearby to sip on if needed. You can also have some light snacks within reach to help keep your energy up or to feed each other. You can also use an oil diffuser to give them room a fresh and soothing scent.

- **Get Yourself Spiritually, Physically, and Mentally Prepared**

Before the massage starts, make sure that you have an open mind and heart. If there is something that is causing you discomfort, it is best to skip that, but it might also be a good idea to work through some of the things that make you feel this way. The biggest discomfort people will often experience is due to self-consciousness and insecurity about certain parts of their bodies. Before the massage starts, you may also want to take a shower or bath. It is best if you do this together, but make sure you avoid sexual interactions during this time. Then stand face to face and stretch to help release tension.

Make sure that you are wearing comfortable clothing. You want to make sure that whatever you have on is loose enough that it can be easily removed. However, doing all of this completely nude would a great option as well. But, tantra is all about a slow accumulation of sexual energy, so it is okay to start with clothes on.

- **Begin by Slowly Building Sexual Energy**

Once you have bathed and stretched, sit down face to face in a comfortable position. You can sit cross-legged, or you can also have your legs over one another in order to help the energy from the erogenous zones to be closer.

Simply stare at one another for at least five minutes. The eyes are the windows to the soul, and this is a big player in tantra. The first few times you do this, you may find it uncomfortable, but carry on and start into one another's eyes as long as you are able to. Once you start to feel all of your tension falling away, you have built a real connection. This is the goal. This is the connection that you need so that you can reveal in tantric sex. Do your best to make sure that you maintain your eye contact during this process.

Starting the Massage

Once you are ready, whoever wants to be massaged first can lay down the prepared surface. There are few simple massage methods that you can use, and they are all beginner-friendly so you can use them right off the bat. You will need to have some massage oil to do these massages.

- **Start on The Back Side**

You will need to add about two tablespoons of massage oil to your hands. Smear the oil over your hands at first and then begin to rub your hands to start help get your palms warm. Once your hands are warm, place your hands on their low back and let your hands slither up their back, over the neck and shoulders, and then back down their back and over the buttocks area.

- **The Hand Slide**

Now that your lover has their back covered with oil start to slide your fingers down their spine, massaging all the way down their low back and over their buttocks. Then move back up to their neck, over their shoulders, and then down their arms and to their fingertips. Do this about five times. As you are doing this, communicate with them, and ask for feedback on how it feels or what they like. If your lover isn't much of a talker, you don't have to push them to talk. You have to remember that this all about giving them a sense of relaxation and wellbeing.

- **Kneading**

This will be an easy motion for anybody who has ever baked bread. Even if you haven't, it isn't that hard to do. All you have to do is squeeze your lover's back and buttocks between your fingers and thumbs in a sinuous motion. Then you will glide your hands to another area of their back and repeat this process over and over until you have kneaded your partner's back. You should move from their neck down to their buttocks. In the fleshier areas of the body, like the buttocks, you can use a bit more pressure, so you shouldn't worry about squeezing it a bit more and spreading the cheeks a bit while kneading.

- **Feather Stroke**

Before you move down to the thighs, stroke the shoulders, arms, neck, back, and buttocks with just your fingertips with an extremely light stroke. This should be done for around five minutes. If you have long fingernails, you can lightly scratch their skin. Do this in circular motions, moving from side to side. You want your light and prickly touch to create sensual eagerness for your lover because they don't know what part you are going to touch next.

- **Foot Caress**

You might need to use a bit more oil for this. Rub your oily hands together and then rub the oil down and across their thighs and calves slowly. Knead the back of their legs as well. Do one leg at a time. The feet, whether you realize it or not, is an erogenous zone, so make sure you give them some considerable attention. Add some extra oil to each foot, rubbing it over the ankles, heels, and between the toes. Using the palms of your hands, slide them along the bottom of your partner's foot a few times. Gently rotate their toes clockwise and counter-clockwise. Then move your forefinger between each toe. Gently pull the toes away from the body.

- **Flip Them Over**

Your partner is probably feeling pleasured after everything you just did to their back, so now you can bring the attention to their front. Have them flip over as you apply more oil to your hands. Smear the oil over their belly and slowly start to slide up their stomach, over their nipples, and then back down to their belly. Continue to do this a few more times. As you do this, it spreads energy into their bodies. If your partner is a female, make sure that you a gentle with her breasts. Men can handle firmer strokes across their chests. You can also knead a man's chest if you want.

Once you have finished massaging your partner, it's your turn to get massaged. Allow the massages to progress naturally and let what happens next, happens. People who are more experienced in tantra and tantric massages will also use yoga poses during their massages. You don't have to use yoga poses in order to have a successful tantric massage.

Tantric Yoga

There are several basic yoga asanas you can practice, as a beginner, or a longtime student, that will when practiced with regular consistency, improve the body's overall wellbeing, and enhance your sexual expansion. Tantric yoga involves performing a vinyasa, which is basically the flowing of one pose to the next in order to complete the asanas in sequence together. A vinyasa truly goes beyond just understanding it as movement between poses, however. Your vinyasa experience will be heightened if you also use these moving moments to be mindful of staying in a meditative state and listening to the subtle cues in your body that help you to expand. If a mantra is part of your practice, or you'd like it to be, it is moving through a vinyasa which cultivates the perfect opportunity for your focus on the mantra.

Tantric Sex Improves Health

Sex is a very healthy operation for humans. If you're unfamiliar with the benefits, sex counts as exercise. It can lower blood pressure, increase circulation, lower stress, lessen pain, and increase heart rate. Sex and orgasm can function as a brain wave stimulation to alter body chemistry, which can immediately affect libido, depression, and anxiety. Sex can even improve bladder control and lower the risk of heart attack and even lower the risk of prostate cancer. Medical research suggests that sex improves health drastically by stimulating blood and oxygen circulation, detoxifying the body, improving breathing and lung capacity, and strengthening the heart and cardiovascular system. Additional medical studies suggest that with as little as two sexual experiences a week, the body produces and releases more immunoglobulin A, which is an antibody that protects the individual from illness. It's even been suggested that a healthy sexual appetite will prolong an individual's lifetime expectancy. Orgasm can assist in alleviating depression and making the individual feel younger. Orgasm can even make individuals look younger because of its massive physical benefits. This is not restricted to the "regular sex" orgasm, in fact, because tantra prolongs orgasm and seeks pleasure in other ways, the physical benefits are increased. Safe and satisfying sex will improve an individual's mood and emotional interactions with others, from your partner to your boss, to your child's teacher. These mood enhancements are the factor behind "the glow" some individuals are reported to carry with them hours and even days after sex. While orgasm is a benefit to either gender, orgasms in females come with an added bonus. Frequent orgasm or prolonged orgasm can help the internal workings of the female body and rejuvenate the body and its organs. Because tantric sex includes the entire body for pleasure, this can increase the benefits of orgasm, without even experiencing what we would traditionally identify as an orgasm. The nervous system and the endocrine system benefit here, as well. Oxytocin levels rise in the body and that will improve an individual's mood, stamina, social skills, and emotional control. With so many benefits to one's health, it's a curiosity that sex is not a regular prescription for those with failing physical or mental health concerns.

Deliberate Breathing

Block out the rest of the world for a solid 5-10 minutes for maximum benefit. While it's nice to practice this exercise in a comfortable and relaxing space, it's possible to implement this in a space that isn't perfect. Doing so will actually only strengthen your resilience to block out distractions and concentrate deliberately for 5-10 minutes. The primary function of this exercise is to regulate a slow and steady breathing pattern of 3-count inhales, and 5-count exhales. It's also suggested that when breathing in, you breathe deeply through your nose, and when exhaling, you do so through the mouth as if you're blowing air out from your lips. By adding this breathing exercise to your repertoire, you'll improve focus and memory and decrease stress chemicals in the body. This exercise also decreases the overall sense of anxiety, lowers heart rate and blood pressure, relieves muscle tension, and improves eyesight. Begin by sitting comfortably in a cross-legged position. If this is somewhat uncomfortable for you, try sitting with a pillow under your tailbone, or consider sitting comfortable with your legs outstretched in front of you. For best results, try to ensure that in whichever way you're sitting, your knees are lower than your hips. This helps with your internal flow of energy. Sit with the palms of your hands facing up and resting on your knees. Bring your thumb and forefinger together. Close your eyes. Focus only on your breathing and how that breathing feels in your body. The idea is to focus so acutely on the practice of breathing that begins to experience the action in a new and awakening way. You take note of how the breath feels entering and exiting, how it feels being held in, how it feels moving through the nose, throat, and lungs. Notice the rise and fall of the lungs. Notice the stretching and retracting of the diaphragm. Your breath should be slow, full, and steady. I may help at first to meter your breathing in order to enjoy the full and deep breaths we are not always used to taking. To do this, practice 3x5 breathing. This is a common breathing technique used in meditation and the practice of mindfulness. Like most breathing exercises, this is designed to guide the individual into a slower frame of mind that most often includes a slowing and calming of the body, as well. When the mind wanders, gently guide it back to the breathing exercise. To practice this exercise: Breathe in deeply as you normally would and exhale. Hold your breathing for a moment on the exhale. Inhale again, but this time, breathe in slowly and steadily for a count of 3 in your head. Hold your breath for a count of 3 in your head. Exhale, but this time, exhale in a slowly and steadily for a count of 5 in your head. Inhale again, slowly, and steadily for a 3-count. Exhale again, slowly, and steadily for a 5-count. Continue this pattern of slow and steady inhales and exhales at a 3-count, and 5-count, respectively. You may opt to continue to hold your breath in between inhaling and exhaling as part of your pattern, but it's not mandatory. Do that which is most comfortable. Your analytical mind should be listening closely to your breathing for any sign of faster or unsteady flow. The analytical mind can also remain focused on the evenness of your counts, trying to maintain the slow and steady flow. After a 5- or 10-minute period, you can slowly open your eyes and readjust to your immediate surroundings. With regular practice of this breathing exercise, you will teach your mind and body that you have the power to bring yourself to this peaceful moment whenever you want. Deliberate breathing is an excellent practice on your own, but to benefit your tantric relationship, you can practice this together. When you practice breathing together, your common goal is to see if you can naturally sync your breathing together. This can mean that your breathing in and out is happening at the same time, or it can mean that there is a distinct syncing of one partner inhaling while one exhales. Don't force the syncing. The exercise is to find your own natural rhythm and then to combine, or weave, that with the natural breathing of your partner, for an organic syncing of breath.

Enhanced Partner Pranayama

If you want to practice deliberate breathing with your partner, but you're looking for something to build an even stronger connection to one another, your breathing exercises can be supplemented or advanced with partner pranayama, which essentially means partner-breathing. The practice of 3x5 breathing is still largely the same. The aim is still to find your own natural rhythm of breath and then to see if this can come into sync with your partner's breath. The difference is in creating an even closer and more intimate physical (but non-sexual) connection with one another. Instead of sitting cross-legged next to or across from each other, you will enhance this position. One person (usually the larger of the two individuals) will sit loosely cross-legged. The other person will sit on the lap so that the two partners are facing each other. The person on top should wrap his or her legs around their partner so that the legs envelop the other person's waist and come to rest behind the bottom person is a very loose cross-legged position. Each partner should gently support the back of the other and find a comfortable balance. Come to a comfortable balance resting on and with each other. Close your eyes and gently bring your foreheads together, touching at your third-eye center. Keep one hand gently on the back of your partner and place the other hand gently over your partner's heart. Staying like this, begin to breathe together and find the point where you both sync up. Remember, this doesn't mean you both need to be taking the same breath in or out at the same time. Breathing can be in sync but opposite as well. As you hold this position with your partner, dedicate all of your attention to listening and feeling your partner's breath. Feel it on their chest and in their back and they inhale and exhale. Become more familiar with your partner's subtle and simple physical movements as it changes and expands and contracts under the breath. Remain here in this attentive moment until you're both comfortably done with the exercise, and gently come apart.

Sun Salutations

There are several versions of the asanas of a sun salutation.

It doesn't matter which you use, or even whether you develop your own out of the asanas you most prefer. What does matter is that you use the movements through these asanas as a slow and deliberate time to focus on the expansion of the body. Sun salutations usually move the individual through a series of five or six poses that are all meant to stretch and awaken the limbs and center of the body. This is called a sun salutation because it's often done in the morning as part of a waking routine, deliberately focused on gratitude and movement of the body's energies to expand and better align with oneself for the day. The poses used in sun salutations are generally basic and able to be done by most anyone either in the traditional sense or modified. Again, there is no necessary preparation, and though it's nice to practice in a comfortable space, you can just as easily practice sun salutations for 5-10 minutes at a rest stop or in the office. This practice is largely solitary, but you can certainly practice with your tantric partner. Again, the goal here is to see whether you naturally sync up with your partner while in the moment, and how well you can maintain that connection with each other naturally. If possible, whether alone or together, practice in front of a mirror. Not only can you get a better sense of whether you're expanding your body in a natural and unforced way, but you'll become more familiar with your physical form and seeing it move.

Tantric Sex And Tantric Sex Positions

Right now, will find out about various Tantric sex positions and procedures that you can use for spicing up your sexual coexistence.

The Sidewinder

This position is enlivened from the yoga position of a similar name, and this procedure takes into account deep entrance. It likewise accommodates the couple to keep in touch. For playing out this position, the lady should rest on her side and supports the heaviness of her chest area with the assistance of her hands. She should lift one of her legs and place it on her darling's shoulder while the other leg is lying on the bed. A variety of this equivalent position is that then again the man can rest behind the lady and enter his partner from behind.

The Yab Yum

The Yab Yum position is viewed as probably the best situation for having tantric sex. It is a genuinely simple situation to perform, and it takes into consideration synchronous climaxes. This position helps in animating quite a few places. Likewise, the man's hands happen to be free right now, he can touch his darling's body however he sees fit, since the couple would confront one another, it takes into consideration enthusiastic kisses also. The man should sit leg over leg on the bed or some other agreeable surface and hold his back straight. The lady should straddle him and fold her legs over his lower back. It takes into account delayed here and there developments that can help the couple in accomplishing an all-around planned climax.

The latch

This posture permits the man to get a decent see his sweetheart's face and the other way around. This is an extremely attractive posture and aids in pleasuring both partners. For playing out this position, the lady should be situated on a high stage like a table or even the kitchen counter. She will then need to recline and adjust her upper-middle and her head with the assistance of her hands by inclining onto her elbows. The man should remain between her separated legs and enter her. This is one represent that doesn't need to be limited to the room and is ideal for an off the cuff cavort.

The butterfly

This method is accepted to allow both the partners to achieve a significant level of rapture and takes into consideration deep entrance. For playing out this position, the young lady should rest on the table so that her butt lies at the edge of the table and the man should help lift her lower back marginally off the table and afterward place both her legs over his shoulders. Her vagina would be free for him to infiltrate while remaining in the middle of her legs. Since her legs are shut together, this fixes the vaginal waterway and gives a tight fit. The man should enter her while her butt is in midair.

The double-decker

This is an amazingly suggestive posture and will help in accomplishing a climax with no problem at all. The man will likewise be given a decent perspective on all the activity that is going on down there, and his hands will likewise have unlimited access to lay with his sweetheart's butt. This position is very enabling for ladies since they have all the control here. For playing out this position, the man should sit on the bed while his legs are collapsed under his body. The lady will then need to confront away from him and place her feet on either side of her darling while her feet are set level superficially to give her some help. When she has brought down herself onto his erect penis, then she will just need to begin moving advances and in reverse or can even decide on a here and there movement. The man should basically kick back and have fun.

The last place anyone would want to be

This is an extraordinary posture since it permits both the gatherings to have a similar measure of control and ooze a similar measure of pressure for having a great sexual encounter. People will have an equivalent balance right now. For playing out this position, the man should sit on the bed and support his chest area with his knees. He will then need to move the lower portion of his legs in reverse and place them marginally separated. The lady will then need to expect a similar position yet she will do as such while confronting ceaselessly from him and her run would be squeezing into his scrotum and her back against his chest. Her legs would be joined and afterward set in the space that is accessible between his legs and the man should enter her from behind. For this situation to be compelling, both the partners should remain as near to one another as could reasonably be expected.

Skiff

This position is a slight adjustment of the lady on top position. Right now, bodies should be situated so that both the partners will find a good pace great take a gander at one another's face while occupied with the demonstration. For playing out this, the man should sit down on a seat that can marginally twist in reverse. The lady will then need to put herself on his lap and afterward place her legs on either side of the seat. The young lady should fire an allover development without anyone else, or her partner can help her by setting his hand under her bum and helping her move in an upwards and downwards way.

The mermaid

This is a somewhat fluctuated adaptation of the butterfly, and it takes into consideration a more solace and better hold. Right now, the man can play with his darling's feet. Remember that feet are viewed as one of the most touchy and erogenous pieces of a lady's body. For playing out this position, the lady should expect a similar situation as she did in the butterfly, however, her butt ought to be propped with the assistance of a pad. Her legs should loosen up and ought to be at a 90-degree edge. The man should stand near the table and infiltrate her.

Tsunami

This posture is very agreeable, and it is a sensual treat. This will knock your socks off. This posture is a slight alteration of the exemplary minister style. Right now, the lady should expect the job that a man, as a rule, does in the teacher style. For playing out this, the man should rest level on his back, and his arms should be put close by. The lady should lie over him, and the man should embed his penis into her vagina. The lady should totally loosen up her legs with the goal that they are resting on his. Her palms ought to be put on his lower arm for giving her some help. The lady will then need to begin moving her pelvis in an upward and descending development.

Lap dance

This is a great posture for a man to encounter his darling's body in the entirety of its magnificence. His hands will be allowed to meander around her body, and he can do what he needs. The lady will face away from him as she would have, had she been giving him a lap move. For playing out this position, the man should sit down on a seat, and his back should be kept straight. The lady will then sit on his lap and parity herself by setting her hands on his upper thighs or even his stomach. She will then need to lift herself gradually and place the backs of her calves and brings down herself onto his penis. Another variety of this would be that the lady should bring down herself onto his penis while confronting her darling and this will give him a serious decent perspective on her bosoms. He can choose to prod and play with them for whatever length of time that he satisfies.

Pretzel

This is another position that is satisfying to take a gander at and even simple to expect. This will cause the couple to feel incredibly attractive. For playing out this position, the couple should stoop before one another. The man should move advances, and the lady will fold her arms over him. The lady will then lift herself up and place her left leg by her darling's correct foot; her foot will confront downwards. The man will then need to put his left leg close to her correct foot. When taken a gander at a couple occupied with this posture, they look like a pretzel, an extremely provocative and mouth-watering pretzel.

The spread

This is an essential and an amazingly hot position. This permits the lady to get incredible delight since it lets her stroke her sweetheart and permits him the entrance to joy her. For playing out this position, the lady should sit at the very edge of the couch or even the bed and spread her legs separated. The man will then need to remain in the middle of her legs and infiltrate her. She can draw nearer to him and kiss him while his hands have the entrance to her full body.

The entwine

This posture looks intense and about difficult to copy, however, then it very well may be pleasurable if it's done appropriately. This posture is tastefully engaging. For playing out this position, the couple should sit near one another and face each other. The man should put his legs on either side of his partner. The lady will then need to lift both of her legs and place them on either side of her sweetheart's sides, under his arms. The man's upper arms will secure the lady's legs, and the lady will then need to lift her upper arms and place them over his elbows. The man will then lift his legs and place them over her hands. This does sound very muddled, isn't that right? All the exertion that goes into it will merit your time and energy.

The G-force

This is maybe one of the most blazing tantric sex presents there is. This is the piece de opposition of all sex presents. The man has full oversight over his darling right now, both the people included will get extraordinary delight from this posture. For playing out this position, the lady should rest on her back on the bed, and the man must bow by her legs. He will then gradually lift her middle off the bed so she's offsetting herself with her head and her shoulders put on the bed. The man can either extend her legs at a 90-degree edge or infiltrate her, or he can likewise pull them separated and place her feet just beneath his chest and enter her.

Feminine Orgasms And Tantra

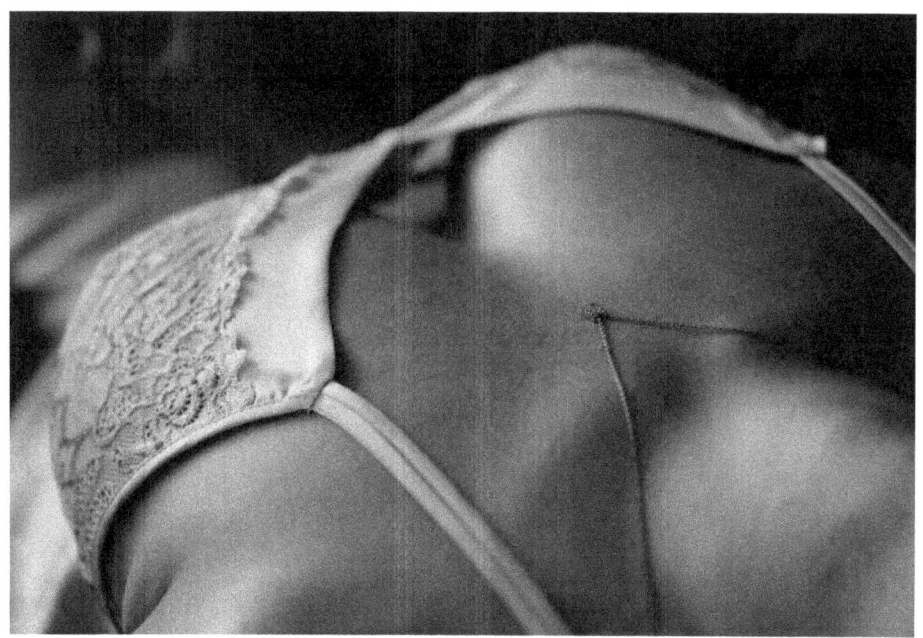

In most literature, it seems that the female orgasm is shrouded in mystery. Some so-called experts claim that it's quite easy to find multiple orgasms. They make it seems as though there is some kind of switch you can simply flip and off you go.

Other gurus make it seem like it some kind of unattainable phenomenon that can only be uncovered by the proprietary method. As such, you stand no chance of achieving orgasm unless you follow their time-tested, patented moves.

The fact of the matter is that the female orgasm works in the same way that the male orgasm does. The female orgasm is an electrochemical reaction that releases all of the chemicals that produce the wonderful feelings that come with having a good time in bed.

However, it is also important to point out that the road to the female orgasm is different. Even if the overall reaction is the same for both men and women, getting it is a bit different. This means that you need to focus on the various components that lead up to the big "O."

In particular, we're going to be discussing the main reasons why reaching orgasm can be difficult. With the ideas that we will present, you'll be able to get a much broader perspective on the limitations that you may be encountering.

Arousal in women

Unlike men, women are not predominantly visual. Yes, women find visual stimulation highly enjoyable. Women value the visual esthetics of an attractive individual as much as men do. The difference is that women do not value visual attractiveness above everything else. In fact, women tend to value visual symmetry a lot more than men do.

When talking about symmetry, it's important to keep in mind that women enjoy men who look proportionate. That is why most women don't find bodybuilders particularly attractive. The same goes for men who are too thin or those who are obese. The secret is maintaining a proportionate look in terms of height and weight. This means that while men don't need a chiseled body to be attractive, trying to maintain proper proportions makes a huge difference.

The way arousal works in women is that you have an overall sensory experience that leads to a set of emotions. It is this emotional connection between sex and emotions that leads to a pleasant sexual experience. In a manner of speaking, if your heart is not into it, then arousal can be hard to pursue.

Of course, there is instinctive arousal which is mainly driven by the need for physical intimacy. However, this need for physical intimacy is often confused with sex. Sadly, culture has reduced intimacy with sex. The reality is that sex is only one part of intimacy. This is why we have made a strong case for the need to incorporate intimacy in your life without making sex the main priority. When you take the need for sex out of the equation, you are left with the entire scene around you. When this scene isn't there, then you have no choice but to build it.

Fostering arousal should then become about creating a safe atmosphere in which you feel comfortable being yourself. Now, this is crucial as feeling uncomfortable, in any way, can be a huge detrimental factor in limiting your ability to enjoy sex truly. When you feel comfortable with yourself and everything you are doing, then you can certainly make things work as best as it can for you.

What's holding you back

Inexperienced individuals tend to relate the inability to orgasm to physiological factors. They believe that there is something physical that affects your ability to orgasm. The fact is that there are many more psychological and emotional factors that affect your ability to orgasm. That's why the exercises in this book have been presented so that you can put yourself in the proper frame of mind. When this occurs, you are able to make yourself feel open and liberated truly. When you find this sense of liberation, you can then go about enjoying yourself to the fullest.

So, what's holding you back?

The fact is that there is any number of issues that can wreak havoc on your mind at any given point. In particular, being uncomfortable with your body can play a largely detrimental role in helping you liberate yourself. You see, we tend to compare ourselves to certain standards all the time. We compared ourselves to "good" mothers, "successful" professionals, or "good-looking" people.

When it comes to you, and your physical appearance, there is no need to compare yourself to anyone else. Sure, you might be keen on improving your physical conditioning and fitness. But that doesn't mean you are not attractive. If your partner values you for who you are, then you already have the most important aspect of attractiveness. This is why it's important to let go of such hang-ups in the bedroom. Being too overly focused on this aspect will limit your ability to enjoy yourself truly.

Also, stress plays a huge factor in holding you back. When stress gets the best of you, it can be nearly impossible to shut your mind off. If anything, you'll be faced with nagging voices in your head that won't leave you alone. You might be really enjoying yourself when you are suddenly hit with a flood of thoughts regarding any number of things. These thoughts can totally undermine your ability to enjoy yourself truly.

To combat this, the breathing and relaxation techniques we have presented are highly effective. Also, making time for yourself and your partner means that you have the freedom to enjoy yourselves without being concerned with other things. Just being able to forget about your phone for a while is enough to get you feeling completely liberated from the world around you.

Another crucial factor is to address any issues that may be driving a wedge between you and your partner. Unfortunately, all couples have issues, especially if they have been together for a while. Often, unresolved issues fester beneath the surface. So, you don't really see them superficially. But below the surface, they are clearly affecting the way you interact with your partner. As such, if there is anything that is affecting your relationship, it's important to deal with it, get it out of the way, and move on. If you let it sit there, it will gnaw at you.

This will become evident as you engage in tantric practices. You might start okay, but if such thoughts should hit you, you won't be able to recover. You'll have no choice to get over it or struggle with them throughout your tantric sessions.

Getting to the big "O"

There is a general misconception that it is hard to get to the big "O." The fact is that it's neither easy nor hard. It's just a question of knowing how to go about it. This implies that when you are committed to the experience you are living, you can find the pleasure you seek. Many times, it's just a matter of getting lost in the moment. This is why we have mentioned the need to live "in the now." When you manage to get everything out of the way, you can find the path to true pleasure and ecstasy.

Unfortunately, the big "O" seems like an elusive target. This occurs when you are completely focused on getting there without really taking in the entire experience. This puts unnecessary pressure on you. After all, why make orgasms the main attraction to sex when there are so many other things happening?

This is an important consideration as sex is filled with various situations and occurrences. You have intimacy, touch, sights, scents, and also your role in giving your partner pleasure. With all of those things happening all at once, there is no reason why you should become fixated on just one.

When you let go of your pursuit of the big "O," you will find that everything becomes much more enjoyable. You won't find yourself completely focused on getting there. Rather, you will enjoy the journey, so to speak. It's a means of enjoying the read even if you don't reach the final destination. Sure, it would be great if you did, but if you don't, it wouldn't be the end of the world.

Something else to consider is that tantra allows you to build up enough experience so that you can learn exactly what buttons to push and when to push them. The various exercises that we have presented throughout this book will enable you to find the right spots for you. This means that you won't have to guess. You'll know exactly where the road will take you. Ultimately, this is a comforting situation as you won't have to doubt or second-guess yourself.

The path to the big "O"

Here is a very simple exercise which you can do to get you to the big "O" every time.

First, think about the road you will be traveling on. This could be a massage, a massage followed by sex, or perhaps just a moment of intimacy with your partner. When you visualize what you are about to do with your partner, it builds anticipation. This anticipation plays a nice erotic game with you as you become expectant of what can happen. When you build up with anticipation, you naturally become aroused. Unless you're not feeling up to it, just the sheer anticipation of a sexual encounter is enough to get your curiosity moving.

Next, see with your eyes what your partner is doing. Take in the sights, sounds, and scents of what's going. This could be a massage, cuddling, or intercourse. It really doesn't matter. The idea is to take in everything that's happening.

Then, close your eyes and try to "see" it in your mind's eye. Try to visualize everything movement, touch, or thrust. In a manner of speaking, you are translating what your body feels to what your mind can see. If you wish, you can limit your visual capabilities. For example, a blindfold or sleeping mask can work quite well.

Since your mind is occupied trying to recreate a visual from what you are feeling, you are more concentrated on taking in the sensory experience rather than actually seeing the events unfold. As you render these images in your mind, you will find that the sensory experience builds up.

After, try your best to anticipate the next move. If you are in control, say in a cowgirl position, try to anticipate your next move. In a manner of speaking, you are planning what to do next as you go. When you do this, you are building up even more anticipation. As such, you are avoiding a mechanical motion by transforming in order to into a fluid movement.

How To Control Ejaculation And Last Longer

Also, men want more pleasure. Which man wouldn't want to take more than two in a row, prevent impotence, and increase the quality of the orgasm?

Pompoir is a set of techniques of oriental origin, used to strengthen and control the muscles of the vagina, usually to increase sexual pleasure. Known widely for its benefits for women, the word Pompoir derives from the Tamil language, spoken in Sri Lanka and southern India, and means mental command over the pubococcygeus muscle, the circunvaginais muscles, and the large labia of the female vulva. But in this chapter, we will see how to do some specific exercises for men that will help increase self-esteem, virility, and self-control.

What Is Pompoir For Men?

Who does not want to reach deeper orgasms, increase pleasure, and prevent disease? These are some of the benefits offered by Pompoir and you will learn the basics here to start having more pleasure and lasting longer.

These sexual gymnastics known by select groups of people in India, Thailand, Indonesia, and other Eastern countries has spread all over the world. This technique has been developed by these people for over 1,500 years.

Although it is usually associated with women the ancient art of Pompoir can also be practiced by men. It promises to expand the quality of sexual life and hot moments together. Pompoir for men is the technique of intimate gymnastics based on regular exercises that help to improve coordination, skill, and muscle strength.

These exercises bring highly significant results to the health of your sexual organs. Increasing your self-knowledge, control, you will know exactly when to stop stimulating, before that point of no return.

Often, speaking of male Pompoir, reference is made to a version close to the female, which includes the introduction of some tools in intimate parts for the development of the practice. But in practice, male Pompoir has nothing to do with it.

The exercises are performed only by stimulating the muscles, contracting, and relaxing, and there is no reason to worry about it. Forget the idea of Pompoir as something feminine and understand all the benefits that this practice can generate for your sexual and daily life.

Male Pompoir is the key to extreme pleasures. To achieve these goals, be patient and kind to yourself, some of the exercises listed below can be reconciled with some daily activities such as driving, sitting in the office, watching TV, and, of course, during sex.

Benefits Of Pompoir For Men

The benefits of male Pompoir are to strengthen the pelvic region, leading to greater blood circulation, allowing the man to have sex for hours, maintaining a stiff erection, controlling ejaculation, and feeling more sensitive. This will make the man last longer and get better orgasms.

For men, the act of Pompoir brings several benefits with practice. First, there is an improvement in sexual performance, that is, the man, in addition to lasting longer, has more vigor. This happens due to the strengthening of the pelvic muscles and the improvement of blood circulation, which increases the effects of erection.

Besides, the exercises ensure greater control of the region, including concerning stimuli and ejaculation time. A man who practices male Pompoir tends to suffer much less with premature ejaculation than others.

The practice also promotes control of other activities, such as attention to breathing and self-knowledge. They may seem small factors, but they are absolutely important for the development of a higher quality of life.

How To Start Practicing Pompoir For Men

First, you should start with adequate breathing throughout the practice. For this, it is important to inhale deeply through the nose. Do this with your abdominal muscles relaxed. Exhale slowly making sure that the movements are always concentrated in the abdomen.

This perception is essential for the control of the body. It allows the diaphragm to be responsible for breathing, which makes the body function properly, without disturbing the muscles to be worked on during the exercise.

The target muscles of male Pompoir are the pubococcygeus muscles. They are located between the male penis and the anus and are the same muscles used, for example, to stop the flow of urine when in the bathroom.

Exercises For The Pubocoxigen

First Exercise - Also known as Kegel Exercise

When urinating, try to contract the muscles to stop the urine flow, repeat it several times. It is normal during the first attempts to feel a burning sensation. If you are able to stop the flow it means that you are on the right track. But don't go overboard.

Second exercise – Muscle knowledge

Sitting in a comfortable place with your spine erect, try to contract the muscle you used to stop the flow of urine. Well, now focus on that region and do short and fast contractions, start with 10 reps and gradually increase. Note that your penis will move during contractions. It is normal for the belly and anal muscles to contract initially, but over time, you should only be able to contract this muscle. Do 3 reps 10 times a day.

Third exercise – Movement control

Standing and naked in front of a mirror, contract the pubococcygeus several times and observe the movements of the penis. The stronger the muscle, the stronger the movements of the penis.

What Is An Intimate Pussy Massage?

An intimate pussy massage includes touching the female genital area (outer lips, inner lips, clitoris, and vagina). If you spend time working up to orgasm via an intimate pussy massage, the results can be wondrous for your partner. This is totally different from self-pleasure or solo masturbation, as you (the partner) would be in control.

And did you know that an intimate pussy massage doesn't have to take place in the bed? Sometimes it's best to start the process of arousal in a totally different setting, all of which will go to heighten the actual orgasmic release! (Like I mentioned before, in the kitchen!)

You can tease your partner in public. Tell her the things you'd like to do to her sexually...in the grocery checkout line, at the cinema concession line, or out shopping at the mall. Getting her wet in public, knowing you can't actually just have sex (I say wait till you are home, quickies in bathrooms are gross!) heightens sexual tension and can be powerful in drawing up her sexual pleasure.

Try this:

- I can't wait until I touch your pussy.
- I love how your pussy feels against my fingers.
- I can't wait to pleasure you until you beg for more.
- I love how your pussy reacts to my fingers when they are inside of you.
- You turn me on so much, you're my goddess and I'm going to make you come.

If you feel nervous about saying these things, then text these thoughts to your partner even if they are right beside you (they do work, let me tell you!). This also works (amazingly) in a restaurant setting on date night. You and your partner are working up a secret sexual storm in a crowded place and it pulls you both intimately together. However, try and keep off your phone when stimulating pleasure or creating a sexy environment.

Why an Intimate Pussy Massage?

Just as a full body massage can rejuvenate you, an intimate pussy massage can relieve and release a huge amount of tension. Does she have a stressful job? Challenging lifestyle or family situation? Then intimate pussy play is a safe, healthy way to let her reconnect back with herself — and you're allowing her to do this in a safe, loving space. You're fostering trust here, iron-clad trust that you see, hear, and know that your woman needs. Put aside your own sexual needs for the moment and pleasure her and the rewards for her can be intense.

How to Perform an Intimate Pussy Massage

If you've spent time building up the energy for the pussy massage time, then you may find your partner is already wet. If not then use some lubricant (always ensure it's suited to you, and always patch test and follow instruction) keep protection handy for any penetration — if that is something that you have decided will happen — however it's not the goal, the goal is her pleasure remember!

Undressing her, while you stay fully clothed is a sexy, sensual act. If you encounter shyness from her (especially if you haven't been together long) take a moment and offer comfort. Our bodies are beautiful, no matter the shape or size but we have been conditioned to forget that.

Try this:

- Your body is stunning.
- I love how you respond to my touch.
- Let me undress you.
- I will take care of you.

Create a haven. Light a candle, keep the light dim, or use moonlight or natural light. Use the shadows or don't use them. Create a soft place to explore her, either a bed or a pillow and blanket fort on the floor. Just be comfortable.

Once she's naked, gaze at her intimate area that you are about to touch. Hold her hands and simply be in each other's presence. Breast and nipple play is encouraged — use light, teasing touches. Being this intimate with someone can often have positive, vibrations in your relationship. It's not all about fast, quick, and hard sex (although that is fun too!) Gazing at her this way is a marvelous way to see the female form and to adore it. Speak what you feel. Tell her how you feel.

Try this:

- Thank you for trusting me.
- Your pussy is beautiful.
- I love her texture, her colour, her juice.
- I want to get her ready for my touch.
- Can I touch you there?
- I love how she's getting wet for me.

Does it Feel Good When I Touch You Here?

With your woman on her back, get as close as you can, this usually means draping her legs over your thighs, as if you want to lock your genital areas together. (If you want to be naked, then go ahead, in case clothing is chaffing, or getting in the way). Start by putting one hand on her heart chakra (just at the middle of her breast bone — a chakra is an energy point) and let the fingers of your other hand caress her inner thighs, working your way to her labia (lips).

What do you notice here? Can you smell her? Speak and create a pleasure route map so she knows what to expect from you. Whisper, rather than shout. Let her know in a voice that she is your queen and you will take care of her. Make sure you are groomed and clean...especially your nails! Nothing too long or too sharp! If you have long hair, tie it back so there's nothing in the way.

Try this:

- I adore you.
- You make my heart full.
- I am lucky to have you in my life.
- Thank you for loving me.
- I adore all that you are.

- You are perfect to me.
- Let me pleasure you.

She might be really wet and could feel embarrassed by "leaking" assure her that there is nothing wrong (use towels if you are worried about the sheets) her genitals will be engorged and may pulse awaiting your touch. Listen to her, what sounds is she making? Please ensure that your cell/mobile phones are out of reach and preferably on silent. This is YOUR time...social media will be there when you finish! (My partner and I have a small basket in the hallway where we leave our phones on silent. It means they were truly out of the way).

Time to Touch to Her

Use gentle, feather-light stroke, passes, and pressure. Go slow here — No exceptions! As this will ramp up the pleasure in increasing amounts and as hard as it might be, avoid the clitoris for now. Also, you might be very aroused at this point, and that is good! Show her how she makes you feel. And if you are getting aroused too (perfectly normal and natural!), try the sentences below:

Try this:

- Look how you affect me.
- Look at what your beauty does to me.
- I am so hard just by looking at you.
- I am so aroused by you.

I loved it when my partner would play with my pussy lips, stretching them a little, moving them around. He would "hunt" for my clitoris with focus... and sometimes he did it and maintained eye contact as he did so. When he touched it or got close, he would use my facial cues or moans as a homing beacon. He became an incredible interpreter of my body and you are going to be able to do the same with your partner — just watch her...it can be that easy!

Start with one finger and build from there, keep finger thrusts slow and measured. Slow and go inch by inch. As you push your fingers in and out, watch her (not her pussy). Keep eye contact for as long as you can. This is a powerhouse move to create intimacy and a long-lasting sense of closeness long after you have left the bedroom. Always insert fingers with gentleness, let her expand naturally. Is she holding her breath? Tell her it's okay to breathe, that you have her safe and secure. The goal here is to get her very wet, bubbling with sexual need and the desire to come.

Intimate Pussy Massage Techniques

The plough

Using alternative fingers enter the pussy then use the other hand's fingers to enter the pussy. Swap them slowly, sensually, and make her miss your touch. Listen to what she's saying, doing. Is her breath changing, her moans getting louder, is she moving around a lot?

Rocking the boat

Using one hand, two fingers is best, insert them into the vagina and rock them side to side, creating a semi-circle shape that goes from east to west, then west to east. (Imagine tracing half a circle, rather than going side to side).

The full O

Just like the rocking the boat technique, do a 360 with your fingers. Keep your moves slow and steady as if you are stirring a pot.

The G spot graze

Use your fingers to search upwards (upper wall of the vagina about an inch or so in) and seek out a small bumpy region. She may squirt when this spot is stimulated over long periods — so just watch her see if this might happen. Imagine the roof of her vagina is the sky and you are gently parting the clouds.

Infinity

Trace the figure eight over her clitoris. Just use one fingertip, and go....slow...this one can have explosive results. Watch her face for clues as to how close she is to orgasm — if you want to deepen her orgasm, back off, maybe play with her nipples or breasts, let her settle, and start the tracing again, edging her ever closer.

Mirror Dancer

Stand or have her sit (on the edge) of a chair in front of a large mirror. You can kneel or sit before her so that she can look at herself. (You can be either in front or to the side, but in front works best as the reflection will be just for her.)

This is almost akin to worshipping your goddess and can make her feel cherished, adored, and safe. I recommended creating a haven in the room, so candles, clean bedding, and so forth. I was given one of my best orgasms ever on Valentine's Night when my partner put a chair at the foot of the bed, undressed me, and used the rock the boat and the full O technique. And he did it without saying a word and kneeled in front of me while I watched myself.

If she has an orgasm...

Hold her at the moment; allow her to move, moan, and to let her fully experience the sensation. You should keep your fingers inside (if you can't then that's okay, let her be the guide), noting how she clenches around you. Keep a finger or two (the pads of your fingertips of your other hand) against her clit, this can result in multiple orgasms. Use a free hand to stroke her nipples and breasts, her throat, down her breastbone, her belly.

If she doesn't orgasm...

Don't panic, you have done nothing wrong! She may need more stimulation, or she's preoccupied with something. Just keep a loving space open for her, like you have been doing.

Try this:

- Shall I change position?
- Where do you want me?
- How can I make you feel good?
- Can I do more for you?
- Do you want to take a break?

Discover Your Own Body And That Of Your Partner

Certainly, you've heard the expression, "the body is a temple," and if this is the first time you've heard it, the meaning is still pretty clear. Treat your body like a temple. As you prepare for your tantric sex experience, this is the rule you will follow.

Prepare your body for your tantric experience by honoring it as a temple. Brush your teeth after taking a hot shower. Groom yourself in ways you know you like, or that your partner likes. Deliberately incorporate things that will stimulate the senses in a very positive way. The sense of smell is possibly our strongest connection to memory. The olfactory system is a powerful subconscious stimulator. Use this to your benefit. Consider applying scents to your temple that are reminiscent of vanilla, rose, jasmine, lavender, white gardenia, orange, citrus, lemongrass, spice, ginger, or just the smell of cleanliness and freshness from soap. These are the scents males tend to be aroused by. Women have an even keener sense of smell than men, so if your partner is a female, consider scents like citrus and spice, musk, sandalwood, rosewood, patchouli, or again, just the fresh and clean smell that comes with stepping out of the shower. Don't go overboard though, or you may create an unpleasant and distracting effect. Give attention to the sensation of touch.

The clothing you wear for your tantric experience should be wonderful to touch and feel on your own skin — luxurious and opulent, such as is worthy of a temple. This clothing should also be loose and comfortable, and simple and easy to remove. Many couples opt for a completely naked experience. Consider preparing your temple to be pleasing to your partner's sight. Wear clothing that is appealing as well as comfortable. Leave the sweatpants and t-shirt for another night and go with something sensual and enticing, but again, not something too restrictive or uncomfortable.

Fix your hair the way you know you like it, or that your partner will like it. Try going into the experience with no makeup and hair products, or very little of each. While you want to smell sensual for your experience, again, don't go overboard. Too much product will have you tasting like chemicals as your lover is trying to experience your body. Stick to light fragrances like essential oils, which have no alcohol in them and will therefore not produce a chemical taste on your flesh.

Take inventory of your body and whether you have any physical pain. If you have an injury or you're experiencing mild pain, it doesn't mean you can't still enjoy the tantric experience. Where regular sex might say, "I have an injury in my left shoulder; let's stay away from using that shoulder," tantric sex says, "I have an injury in my left shoulder; let's please give extra attention and care to this area." If you or your partner have a particular pain or injury, don't leave it out of the experience, bring it in. Allow your partner to offer you gentle massage and care with respect to this part of the body. Rather than ignoring this part of the body, you are healing it.

When your temples are prepared, come together in your sacred space. Begin with an opening ritual for your tantric sex. This solidifies in the subconscious mind that something very unique is happening, and it works as a form of hypnosis to more easily bring you both into the right alignment each time you practice it. A common way to open your ritual is to offer praise to one another. A physical aspect of the ritual will work well, too.

Begin every tantric sex experience together with something to mark the transition. For example, consider as you each start, bow to one another, just as you would bow in a temple. If this doesn't feel right for you, consider starting with a long embrace, or by kissing the backs of each other's hands. If you're incorporating music, begin a piece of music and sit together, across from one another, and listen to this music while you make eye contact. This is a good time to start syncing your breath together, and the music and eye contact will help.

Preparing for Tantric Sex – What You Need to do

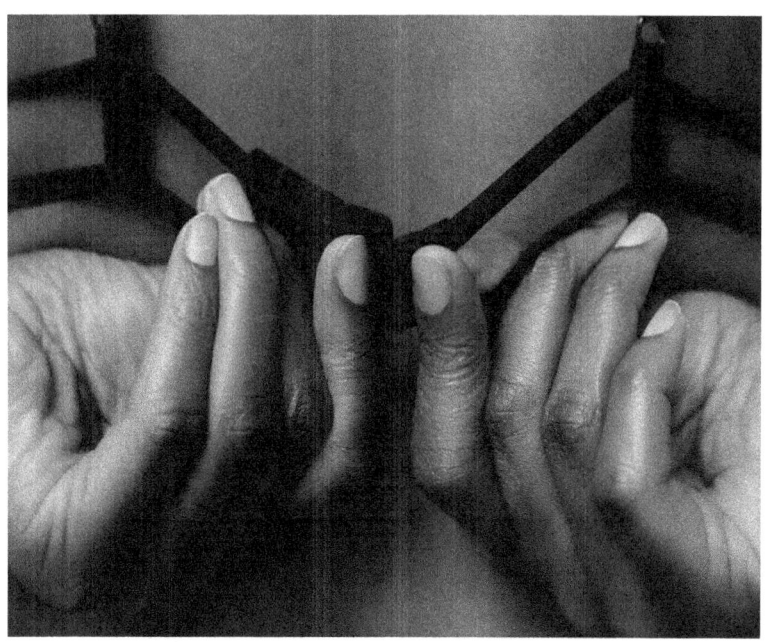

Now that you know about the benefits of tantric sex, and you feel like you're ready to try it, here, we'll discuss how to prepare for tantric sex and what you need to do to prepare to engage and enjoy tantric sex with your partner.

Talk to Your Partner

Before you begin with this, always make sure that you and your partner both want to try this. Remember, it takes two to tango, and that goes for tantric sex, especially. If you're interested in doing it, you need to make sure that your partner is on the same page as you are. Most people don't realize that this is something that your partner may not be ready for.

While you think starting right away is a great idea, but here's the thing: you have to, with tantric sex, discuss this since it is a two-part procedure and something that you'll have to do together. If you're both not interested or working together, it won't happen.

Plus, if you're practicing tantric sex, but they're not, it would mean only one of you is going to experience powerful orgasms and want to take it slower, while the other will be doing the opposite. It seems a little bit unfair, right? That's the main issue you run into with tantric sex if you experience it any other way, it's that you're not going to make it work, and you won't get the results.

And it shouldn't be hard to convince your partner to try it. After all, you want deeper intimacy between you and the other person, better sex, more passion, and just more fun between the two of you.

This is simple to get your partner's agreement on since it is probably something they'll enjoy from the spicing up and variety alone.

Prepare the Body

Preparing the body is a good thing to do with tantric sex because it takes time. Frequently, people don't realize that tantric evenings can be a bit physically demanding. It frequently also makes you feel better about yourself too. You'll appreciate the way your body feels and the wellness you experience.

When you feel good physically, and the room is arranged how it should be, it'll tranquilize you, making lovemaking some of the best there is.

So what are some things that you can do? Well, first and foremost, if you're not someone who wants to spend hours at the gym or work too hard on their physical fitness, then try yoga.

Yoga is one of the best choices that you'll experience. It is a great thing that will help with improving your experience.

Not only that, but yoga also helps with flexibility, and some postures will change your sex life too. Some of them can even be used during tantric sex. Plus, it helps with realigning the energy.

It's deduced that energies you have flowed from your spine, so you should always make sure that you have a relaxed back that isn't hunched over. You should also do this n a way where you're not hurting yourself, and it isn't physically affecting the back.

Diet Tips

Diet is the next area to focus on. Diet is actually on par with physical fitness, but for tantric nights it also helps improve them. Diet doesn't mean you have to follow a complex menu that some guru put together, but what you should do is eat in a manner that's healthier than ever. The best way to do it is to have healthy habits and practice moderation. Try to abstain from overindulging as you get closer and closer to the tantric night. You should try not to eat a lot of heavier foods right before having tantric sex, and also don't overconsume alcohol either.

You should stay hydrated, but also not drink a ton of water too much once you get closer to time. That's because you want to keep things steamy, and while bathroom breaks happen, you don't want that hindering everything.

Also, look for safe detox recipes, with the focus being on safe. You should look for ones that have happy users and those who have some complaints so you could also look at the difference between them.

Don't look for reviews that are overly happy either. That's because happy reviews are faked, but the negative ones aren't either. But you should also look at safety concerns too. If you have a condition that's also affecting your ability to do a diet, also research the side effects of that.

You should also try to snack minimally, and if you do snack, you should also be mindful of what you're eating. There's a lot that you can eat that's healthy and good for you, and a lot that you should minimize. Go through and look for all of these, so you can better understand what you're doing, and also don't overindulge in these as well. Because let's face it, do you need to gorge on those cookies? Probably not.

Relaxing the Body

Before you get into tantric sex, you should try to relax the body. Relaxing the body is very important because if you're not relaxed, you're going to feel a bit exhausted and probably sick from the stress. After a bad day, even if you didn't do a whole lot, it'll feel like you've fought with a bear and lost.

The body is important to relax, but you should also make sure that you relax the mind too. Mental stress does weaken your immune system, and bacteria and viruses love when that happens.

Learning to relax is a possible thing, but the big thing to remember here is not to float around like you're in a Zen haze. You might live in a chronic-stress situation, though, and that becomes the new normal for many. Lots of times, people don't realize how stressed out they are, and the debts, demands, and coping skills frequently are a reason why people drift apart. This is a big thing to understand because tantra helps you build a bond that's closer than ever before, that's more than just sex for many people.

Frequently, relaxing is a hard-pressed concept. You probably might have issues with a long-term stress reliever, but a nap, a shower, or a funny movie is helpful. Meditation is valuable, but it's an overlooked thing, but you need to learn to accept that you're stressed out, and you need to spend time preparing yourself for this. If you're a bit sad about the way that you look, try to spend 30 minutes maybe a day walking or working out. It does bring about liberation to you in its way. Plus, if you're relaxed, you'll practice tantra way better, and accept all of this in the long run.

What to Wear

Some people think that you need to wear very tight and sexy clothes. No, wear something loose, comfortable, and you should try to put something on that makes you feel good. Some people will dress in attire that reflects certain deities or the east. But it can help bring about the art of tantra into the bedroom

However, you should also focus on being clean and happy with yourself before you practice tantra.

First, brush your teeth and hair before you do. This is a quick and simple thing to bolster your confidence and make it easier for you to do as well.

Some people like to do a ritual bath beforehand, but that is something that you don't have to do. You should make sure that it's a bit structured, and that you have the aim of making sure that you are bonded, but not bonded enough to have sex yet. You should wash one another in ways that are on-sexual and use soaps and oils that are scented. This fosters anticipation between the two people, and it's something that you'll enjoy with the other person.

You should do things together that foster anticipation between both of you as well. That will, in turn, benefit both of you, and it does bring about a good and artful experience with your partner.

Setting Your Scene

You should set the scene up by putting rituals into sex, and make sure that your space is set up. Most people focus on making sure there's a lot of white in the room, such as in the form of pillows, candles, and also soft music. You should do this with the intent of making the sex feel special.

For most people, they just rush into the bedroom and don't work to set the mood. But, if you want to make it memorable for both parties, you should try decorating it. Soft, sensual music will help bring forth a better, more intimate experience between both of you. Music is excellent for sex period, but gentle, sensual music will change the way sex is for both parties and brings forth a sense of understanding, wellness, and happiness as well.

Breathe Away!

Before you even start, you should breathe and make sure that you do it in a way that benefits you. This is a good way to calm yourself down mentally and to help you relax. What you should do is take one full breath in through the nose, fill the belly with air, and then exhale. You should notice your belly move outwards. That's your diaphragm breathing, and you should make sure that you do focus on getting that type of breathing. When you exhale, you should see the belly start to return to normal size.

If you're having issues with this, you should visualize that pushing the pelvis down through there, and you push the breath directly to the floor. Try to do this a few times before you do it during sex, so it becomes more automatic so that you can benefit from this too.

Try Massages

Finally, before you have sex, you should try massaging. These massages don't have to be a long time, but you should try to switch off between the giver and the receiver of leisure. You might ask your partner to rub your feet for a couple of minutes, and then do whatever they like for a couple of minutes.

During each turn, don't be afraid to give the feedback that you need to. It's okay to tell your partner what it is they should do better, and this will help them give you what you want.

This is something most couples struggle with. By talking to the other person, you will be able to get what you want. Communication is something that most people need to understand has to be there. The way you work together is a great way for you to learn. You will be able to teach your lover what you want, and they'll teach you what they want, creating the best sexual experience possible for you.

Tricks and Tips

Tricks

Trick#1: Exploration of your senses

Tantra is an ancient art that has been around for centuries. It is essential to remember that tantra is not just about improving the quality of your physical intercourse but it is also about the emotional experience. Even your various sensory organs take part in the process of having sex. So, tantra is also about improving the experience of all your senses, touch, sight, smell, taste, and sound. It has been proven that once any of your senses has been compromised, the rest become more sensitive.

You can use this as an inspiration and probably make use of it to experience sex with your partner in a manner that you have never tried out before. It is not just essential that you are participating in the intercourse, but it is also important that you are able to explore all the senses of your partner. You both should be able to create an atmosphere that is conducive to this, an environment that can ignite your sexual fires.

Don't try too hard, just focus on creating an environment that is relaxing, intimate, and sensual. You might even try blindfolding your partner; this will help stimulate their other sensory organs. For tantalizing their olfactory receptors you can make use of vanilla extracts or even essential oils. Maybe play some music they enjoy or if you want to take a more romantic route may be read out a poem to them. If not reading an erotic story might be a good idea too. Coming to their sense of taste, you can try feeding them such luscious berries or even chocolate, try licking off some whipped cream from their fingers. For arousing their receptors responsible for identifying touch, you can tease their body by caressing them with silk or even feathers. Let your imagination run wild. Once you have teased all their senses, you should remove the blindfold and let them see what you have been up to, and surely your partner would not miss the look of passion and desire in your eyes. It might sound a little drawn out, but the results will be worth the effort that you put into it.

Trick#2: Aim for a full body orgasm

Who doesn't want to have an orgasm, and the sound of full body orgasm might seem more than tempting. So without wasting any time, let me explain the concept of a full-body orgasm. One manner in which you can condition your body to have a full body orgasm is by practicing the build-up to an impending orgasm and then letting it subside without getting yourself off. This means that you will have to drive your partner to the brink of an orgasm and then let it fade away. Once you let it subside, you will have to build it up again and let it fade away again. Use your willpower and keep playing at it for as long as you can and like.

You can take your partner to the brink of an orgasm orally or through any other method, but you should not give them the relief they want, at least not for a while anyway. Keep building up on this pleasure. Because once you do let go of it, the orgasm your partner will achieve will be nothing short of spectacular.

Trick#3: The journey counts

Orgasms are brilliant, but Tantra is not just about achieving orgasms, it is about delaying your orgasm for a while to achieve results that will help you attain a higher level of sexual awareness of not just yourself but your partner as well. Understandably, the fun of engaging in sexual intercourse might be taken away by the stress of having to achieve a pleasurable result. This stress is not a good thing and it will have a negative impact on a person's performance. Enjoy the journey; it is as important as the end result itself. And Tantra will help make this a fun activity again. If you keep running behind the aim of achieving only an orgasm, likely, you might just bore your partner and you both might get stuck doing the same thing over and over again. Try enjoying the process of having sex. Try focusing on things that you enjoy and also the things that your partner enjoys. There will certainly be certain things that you both enjoy. Find those common things; it might be kissing, foreplay, holding each other or any oral activity. Explore the likes and fantasies of your partner. The results will be truly favorable.

Tips

The thigh-high

Select any of your favorite scented oils and squeeze a few drops of it in your hands. Now place these well-oiled palms on your partner's thigh, a little above their knees. Start kneading gently, the way you would be wringing your towel. Now make your way northwards, but slowly. Let the anticipation build along with the sweet sexual tension. When you finally reach the area near the groin, do not actually touch your partner's genitals; instead, work the muscles surrounding this region.

Take the nail road

Use your nails and trace patterns of figure eight on your partner's inner thigh and run your nails along the length of their calf and thighs. Try tickling the arch of their foot; it is very sensitive to touch. Try changing the pressure slightly and keep them guessing.

Try the aural sex rub

Try massaging your partner's ear, but do it very gently with fleeting touches. Use your fingers and work the outer fold of the ear and make your way downward. Run your little or your pinkie finger along the crease of their ear, the point where this point joins their head. Now let us build the anticipation a little more and you can gently lick the inner ear with your tongue, prod slightly.

Now, turn up the heat

Now it is time to turn up the heat. There are different ways in which this can be done. One easy method would be to slip either some luscious berries or even chocolate back and forth between you and your partners while kissing. You need to include things that would tantalize their sense of taste and touch as well. You can try spilling some champagne and let it bubble down their body while you are licking it off. Even some whipped cream would come in handy.

After these steps, you and your partner must be overflowing with sexual anticipation. And this is where the principle of tantra, to build anticipation and cool it down, comes into picture. It is all about working up the build of sexual arousal to the brink of an orgasm and then letting it fade away. You have to drive your partner to the peak of pleasure and let it subside. You can do this multiple times. Keep doing this till you both can handle it. The more the sexual tension is the more satisfying the relief will be. The longer you make it last, the climax is going to be that much better. Don't think about gratifying yourself immediately. Instead, focus on making the journey last longer. Let yourself go to the brink of an orgasm, but don't let go just yet. Wait for a while and then when you do let go, the orgasm will literally take your breath away.

Conclusion

In conclusion, tantric sex is one of the best things in the world, but please do not try it until you are at least forty years old. When you are young and overeager, it can really fuck you up. However, when you have learned your way around the world for a while, maybe you can try it. But do it right, and have so much fun. Just go to the thrift store, grab some seventies clothing, and go fuck yourself. Cheerio.

Tantric sex enables couples to have a spiritual connection while talking dirty. it gets the most out of the experience because the couple focuses on pleasuring the senses during sex and delaying the orgasm until the most exquisite one. During that period, it is possible to experience the four levels of orgasm. it is a road a couple can go down during sex, only to return to the ordinary, if desired. In tantric sex, the orgasm occurs in stages.

When you have mastered tantric sex, you can see both of your partner's faces from the corners of your eyes. For a married couple, this can perpetuate a variety of hallucinations. This is what it must feel like to be in an outback of a convent in Australia. You can see the clock ticking from the other side of the world, like a compass pointing south.

For a single person, the sensation is fascinating. If the couple is top and bottom, an orgasmic experience occurs while watching, their bodies undulate. The bottom figure goes "dead" for a second while the top figure grips the bottom figure, trying to pull it to the top. The orgasm is so intense it is impossible to scream out. You cannot even moan. The body has to fill itself with air to provide the necessary vibrating to get as close to an observation point as possible.

The process is like a television screen. You are at the part of the girl holding the guy, and then you're up at the ceiling, looking at your bodies from another location. Either hallucination is fascinating for those who have never experienced it.

You have probably already known about the first orgasm or sexting. it happens when the receiver gets so close to the sender, that the first orgasm can be experienced via the vibration it causes. it can be loud, or quiet. Before the first orgasm, there is just love. After the first orgasm, there are two.

After the initial orgasm, there is a period of ecstasy. The couple can endow their bodies to come again. The woman can lift her body up, reaching out and touching the air, as if it is the man's penis. This period of frigidity is filled with the acknowledgment of the self...

Finally, tantric sex is like psychotherapy. it is a ceremony that explains the condition of a person. in this way, you can experience the conditions of the earth, as well as your own. Every session of tantric sex can be used as a self-defense mechanism. it can be erotic or like a meditation. Every time a couple does it, there is a piece of the universe being lost, and that completes the cycle. Having tantric sex prepares you for the end of the world. You will know to use your body as a weapon.

Tantric sex is awesome--it is just that it's awesome in the wrong way.

www.ingramcontent.com/pod-product-compliance
Lightning Source LLC
Chambersburg PA
CBHW071527080526
44588CB00011B/1588